D1233065

SOCIAL RESEARCH IN CONFLICT WITH LAW AND ETHICS

Recent court cases and legislation involving the rights and responsibilities of researchers accentuate the deepseated tension in this continuing conflict between social critics and vested interests. How can researchers obtain maximum access to information? What is the role of the state in making access more (or less) readily available? Do researchers need protection against compulsory testimony and, if so, what should be the scope of that protection? Should they have immunity from legal liability, especially criminal prosecution, in the course of their work? Do the proposed remedies to current problems imply greater difficulties in the future? These and related questions are here reviewed by a panel of internationally known scholars from the fields of social science and law. Their essays carefully examine legislative proposals, the role of professional associations and possible methodological solutions.

Paul Nejelski, a graduate of Yale Law School, is currently the Assistant Executive Secretary to the Connecticut Judicial Department and lecturer at the University of Connecticut Law School. At the time of the conference he was director of the Institute of Judicial Administration and an adjunct associate professor at the New York University School of Law. Mr. Nejelski was previously a member of the U.S. Department of Justice for six years, serving as a prosecutor and later as the head of a criminal justice research center. He has co-authored several articles on the need for a scholar's privilege including: "A Researcher-Subject Testimonial Privilege: What to Do Before the Subpoena Arrives" 1971 *Wisconsin Law Review* 1085 (1971), and "The Prosecutor and the Researcher: Present and Prospective Variations on the Supreme Court's *Branzburg* Decision," 21 *Social Problems* 3 (special issue, 1973).

Social Research
in Conflict with
Law and Ethics

Social Research in Conflict with Law and Ethics

Paul Nejelski
Editor

Ballinger Publishing Company • Cambridge, Massachusetts
A Subsidiary of J.B. Lippincott Company

This book is printed on recycled paper.

International Standard Book Number: 0-88410-228-9

Library of Congress Catalog Card Number: 76-19082

Printed in the United States of America

Library of Congress Cataloging in Publication Data

Main entry under title:

Social research in conflict with law and ethics.

  German ed. has title: Forschung im Konflikt mit Recht und Ethik.

  Papers presented at a conference held Mar. 1974 at the University of Bielfeld and sponsored by the Center for Interdisciplinary Studies of the University of Bielfeld.

  1. Social science research—Law and legislation—United States—Congresses.
2. Social science research—Law and legislation—Germany, West—Congresses.
3. Government information—United States—Congresses. 4. Government information—Germany, West—Congresses. I. Nejelski, Paul A. II. Bielefeld. Universität.

Library of Congress Cataloging in Publication Data

Zentrum für Interdisziplinäre Forschung.
Law   340.1'15   76-19082
ISBN 0-88410-228-9

Dedicated to my parents:
Leo and Rena Martin Nejelski,
social scientists, teachers, and good companions

Contents

Preface

The problem explored in these pages is sufficiently complex to inhibit a casual reader from attempting, in any brief summary, to capture its essence. In this prefatory comment, I shall accordingly single out a few facets that caught my attention, confident that other readers of the book will find, in its rich and varied chapters, aspects of equal interest to them.

One point is clear: we shall soon have to face an emergent set of problems arising with increasing urgency at the intersection of law, social policy, and social research. Converging at that corner are several interests; among them are the need to avoid invasions of privacy, the need to obtain information for the enforcement of norms, and the need for society to understand the impact of social policy. The activities of empirical social scientists are, in one way or another, potentially relevant to all of these needs.

Privacy invasion via social policy research represents a danger that varies with the research method and with the problems studied. The danger of invading privacy perhaps reaches its maximum where the behavior studied is contemporary, individual, highly motivated, and contrary to a prevailing norm or law. Much empirical social science policy research is concerned with such activity.

In consequence, the subjects of such research are placed in jeopardy, not only by the danger of privacy invasion but also by the threat that their conduct, thus revealed, may subject them to criminal sanction. Suppose, for example, a researcher wishes to learn how much actual law-breaking behavior has occurred in a cohort of youngsters, in a set of parolees, or in a sample of taxpayers. Would the research be able to answer such questions without incidentally acquiring information that could contribute to the conviction of some of the research subjects? If not, what responsibility does the researcher have both toward the subjects and toward those authorities who are responsible for detecting and sanctioning violations of the criminal law?

In order to meet these problems of privacy invasion and disclosure of criminal evidence, several questions must be addressed. Social science researchers need to be able to probe for information, but not to inflict undue harm. How should that line be drawn? When is it legitimate to use "unobtrusive measures" which avoid the problem of distortions of behavior due to subject self-consciousness? When should the subject of research be informed so that consent may be granted or denied? If consent is required, how detailed an explanation ought to be given (to what kinds of subjects?) of the nature, purposes, and uses of the research? If such an explanation is insufficient to warn the individual of the possible personal consequences of the research, may the individual be considered properly informed? If the disclosure is, by contrast, complete and detailed, might it not significantly diminish or destroy the utility of the research by providing the subjects with an interest in, and a commitment to, a particular outcome?

The problem of inculpatory evidence emerges directly from privacy invasion and its potential solutions. Even if observations are unobtrusive, the social scientist may be reluctant to participate in the process of inculpation. The researcher's role is to observe, to understand, to explain, and perhaps to provide a basis for systematic problem solving; it is not to monitor, to expose, to investigate, to detect, to inculpate. To blur the distinction between these roles— social researcher and police detective—may erode the research role by undermining the core conception on which it is based.

If, in addition, we require social policy researchers to testify in criminal proceedings, even after consent has been given by the subject, the danger of undermining the researcher's role becomes even more severe. When consent is obtained, the researcher characteristically vouchsafes some pledge of confidentiality. Such a pledge may not, in the present state of the law, be honestly made unless the researcher is prepared to undertake extraordinary measures to keep his or her promise.

Among other requirements, the researcher may be forced to contemplate breaking the law—for instance, by destruction of evidence or by contempt of court—if that proves to be the only way to keep inculpatory evidence from the authorities. For the researcher who is not thus prepared or who might be unable to avoid disclosure, it will not suffice, ethically, to hedge or to be silent on the issue. If the subject assumes or is told that data will be confidential, should there not be some effort to qualify that confidentiality with reference to its potential use in criminal proceedings? Yet such a warning might well destroy the accuracy of the data subsequently obtained.

In light of these difficult questions, it is easy to see why Nejelski and Peyser lean toward legislating a researcher-subject privilege. Such an approach would seem to provide realistic protection of the relationship so that subjects could honestly be assured of confidentiality even against the power of subpoena. There remain, of course, many problems to be solved, many terms to be defined, many considerations to be taken into account before such a privilege will be widely accepted. But Nejelski and Peyser have done us a service in proposing such a solution because of the debate it will foster as well as the prospect it affords for a potential solution.

There is an understandable reluctance to extend confidentiality-bearing privileges beyond their present scope. This negative attitude has become manifest in the reaction of courts and legislatures to privileges asserted by newsmen. Extension of a research privilege may well be seen as even more problematic especially given the difficulty of defining and limiting the categories of "researcher" and "subject." To overcome a negative predisposition it will be necessary to make an affirmative showing of need.

The likelihood that such a privilege will be accepted may well depend therefore on the perception among our decision-makers of the importance of the research that results. Why risk protecting research subjects who are guilty of crimes if social policy research doesn't help solve problems? Most of the authors and readers of this book will believe, as I do, that such research is presently and prospectively helpful in solving policy problems. But the contributions of social research to policy solutions could obviously be greater. We should strengthen those contributions, see to it that they are more widely understood, and show the relevant decision-makers how these contributions depend on confidentiality for the success of such work. Paul Nejelski and his colleagues deserve our thanks for having made a good start in that direction.

Dean Richard D. Schwartz
School of Law
State University of New York
at Buffalo

August, 1976

Introduction

A group of interested persons from the United States and the Federal Republic of Germany met at the University of Bielefeld in March 1974 to discuss the conflict of social research with law and ethics. The backgrounds of the approximately twenty-five German and ten United States participants were primarily in law or social science.

The conference was sponsored by the Center for Interdisciplinary Studies (Zentrum Fur Interdiszplinare Forschung) of the University of Bielefeld. A German-language edition of the conference papers, entitled *Forschung im Konflikt mit Recht und Ethik*, edited by Albin Eser and Karl F. Schumann, was published in 1976 by Ferdinand Enke Verlag Stuttgart. In the United States, a grant from the Russell Sage Foundation provided funds for the transcription of the proceedings, translation of the German papers into English, and the writing of a summary of the conference.

Professor Albin Eser, then of the faculty of the University of Bielefeld and now at the University of Tuebingen, was co-chairman with me for the conference. I owe him a special debt of gratitude for his scholarship, enthusiasm, and patience.

Court cases and legislation in both countries involving the rights and responsibilities of researchers helped bring the questions before the conference into sharp focus: How can researchers obtain maximum access to information? What is the role of the state in making access more (or less) readily available? Do researchers need a protection against compulsory testimony and, if so, what should be the scope of the protection? Should researchers have immunity from legal liability, especially criminal prosecution, in the course of their work? Do the proposed remedies to current problems give the promise of even worse difficulties in the future?

Over two years have passed since the conference, but the ideas contained in the papers and summary retain their vitality. The conflicts described herein such as the tension between social critics and vested interests are deep-seated. Indeed, intervening events have underlined the arguments made here. For example, in November 1975 Attorney General Edward Levi amended the federal guidelines governing the issuance of subpoenas to newsmen to include researchers. It is to be hoped that this book will bolster this tentative experiment and provide a basis for legislation and court decisions at both the state and federal levels.

The book is divided into three sections. The first is an introduction to the problems presented in the form of a summary of the discussion at Bielefeld. This summary concludes by reviewing the arguments for and against giving researchers a special status. It contains a tentative proposal for government-established review panels that might control the giving of any special status such as immunity or a testimonial privilege. Next, the ten papers prepared for the conference are divided between (1) those which describe and raise the issues about the conflict, in particular past government attempts to regulate research, and (2) those which focus on solutions through methodology and professional associations, as well as constitutional and legislative responses.

The papers represent a broad experience in social science and law. As a criminologist, Marvin Wolfgang is particularly sensitive to violations of the criminal code in conducting research, and the description of his own problems and soul-searching with a specific research project makes a good opening chapter. Sociologist Gideon Sjoberg next focuses on the need for transnational values in order to explore the hidden side of bureaucracies. Carol Barker, a political scientist with a concern for foreign relations, reviews the classification system, which epitomizes and legitimates government secrecy. As a clinical researcher in biomedicine, Dr. Robert Levine describes some of the tensions between government regulations and research that are pertinent to social science, because biomedicine often overlaps social research (e.g., evaluations of methadone maintenance programs) and because it may be a precursor for government regulation of social research.

Commencing the section emphasizing possible solutions, psychologist Robert Boruch describes statistical and other methodological means of safeguarding research data. Criminologist-law professor

Gerhard O.W. Mueller emphasizes the many roles of the researcher and calls for professional associations to increase their activity. Sociologist Eliot Friedson studies the importance of confidentiality in conducting social science research; he would predicate any special status on the need to protect confidential relationships. Judge Jack Day weighs the First Amendment with competing concerns and opts for a constitutional protection of the free flow of ideas. Constitutional law professor Vincent Blasi compares and contrasts the needs and legal status of newsmen with social science researchers, concluding that researchers need more protection than newsmen. As a former prosecutor turned research administrator, I have drafted a model statute that would create a testimonial privilege for all social science researchers.

> **Paul Nejelski**
> Amesville, Connecticut
> April 1976

Social Research
in Conflict with
Law and Ethics

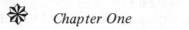 *Chapter One*

Conference Summary

Paul Nejelski

ACCESS TO INFORMATION

Conflicts between law and social research are symptomatic of a relatively free society. It is doubtful that there are similar problems on a continuing basis in Communist countries where each citizen (and researcher) is expected to support the state and contribute to the greater good as defined by its political leaders. When social science is too closely allied with the power structure, there will not be any conflict.

Researchers outside of government control are potentially always in conflict with the establishment. They are agnostics; they threaten the power of the gods; they expose harsh reality. To that extent, conflicts between research and the law are indications of a vigorous, healthy social science.

Before noting the negative aspects of these conflicts, it should be emphasized that most research projects are carried out without serious difficulty. The survey conducted at the University of Bielefeld found that 13 percent of the researchers surveyed—primarily criminologists—had experienced difficulty in gaining access to information or had the confidentiality of their research data threatened. Of these 13 percent some were able to continue the research after making modifications in their research design or objectives.

One American social scientist described his good luck in obtaining access to almost every aspect of the criminal justice system in his city—police, courts, and corrections. His experience suggested that the smaller and more disjointed the system, the easier it is to obtain data. In contrast, a highly centralized bureaucracy such as the Federal Bureau of Investigation is completely closed to outside view.

In the future, researchers will have to be more forceful in their demands for access. They should not worry about getting lost in a jungle of laws and administrative regulations. For instance, a German constitutional lawyer noted that there is a strong tradition in Germany of governmental and civil-service secrecy. Government officials have broad discretion in granting access. German researchers will have to be taught a new basic ground rule: "If the researcher does not do anything on his own and does not start asserting his rights, then of course the civil servant can not be diverted from his traditional mode of thinking."

In contrast, those at the conference who conduct empirical social research were skeptical about calls for increased vigor in attempting to obtain data under present conditions. Information is often perishable. Struggles through official channels have proved costly and not very rewarding. Generally, the researcher has very limited resources available to him; the nature of the work, such as participant observation, is often time consuming or physically exhausting. Legal restrictions or official harassment often make a difficult job impossible.

Even where there is a "right" to access, bureaucracies develop self-protective practices. The researcher may be inundated with so much material that it takes weeks or months to ferret out what is really important. There can be a long delay in granting material, during which the researcher loses heart and the project is damaged irrevocably. There can be sloppy records which produce no information.

The researcher should not have to fight tooth and nail for every piece of information. If the researcher is forced into an adversary role, the burden should be put on the government or private bureaucracy that is resisting access to demonstrate why information should be withheld.

If access can be maximized, then there is much less need for a testimonial privilege or immunity from criminal or civil liability. Granting greater access would be a better political approach, i.e., be more easily obtained from legislatures. It will be difficult for researchers, who are viewed as members of a small and antidemocratic elite, to win special favors. Instead, there is a growing sentiment favoring the opening of organizations to public scrutiny— both government and private bureaucracies. The best example of increased access is the Freedom of Information Act in the United States.

Given this background, the current balance-of-power relationships provide two serious limitations on research. First, the types of research and subjects to be studied are seriously circumscribed. Second, only certain researchers will receive "the royal favor" of access.

Limitations of Subject

As long as the researcher is looking downward in society (i.e., studying the powerless, the defenseless, the lower orders), access will be less of a problem. The minute he begins to look upward in society and study the bureaucracies that control the lives of the average citizen, access becomes much more difficult. In the past, researchers have been content to study the people in lower social and economic strata—even to the point of romanticizing some of their subjects, such as criminals. Persons in the lower social orders have been subjected to so many different types of authority that they feel they are expected to respond to whoever comes in and asks questions, including researchers.

Even in the case of research subjects from "powerless" groups, the situation is becoming more complex. Some of the traditional subjects of research, e.g., blacks in the United States, are organizing to restrict access by researchers and to control the researcher-subject relationship in ways which they feel will be more favorable to themselves—e.g., there must be a black researcher on the project, or black researchers must review and comment on the results before they can be made public. Further, there is a growing concern about the right of these "defenseless" members of society not to be researched.

The accessibility of major private and governmental power structures constitutes a major problem of social science in the future. There have not been many conflicts in the past because social scientists have not yet touched the most sensitive areas. They have only begun to study the most powerful bureaucracies. To the extent that research is a function of those who pay for it, researchers are the agents of these poweful bureaucracies. In the past, social scientists interested in criminology had to be content with studying the criminal and his behavior. Now, the trend is to study the organizations of social control as well—the police, the courts, the correctional institutions, the treatment programs—and subject them equally to the harsh light of investigation.

A German social scientist gave the example of his attempts to study police interrogation of juveniles. The police summarily refused any access, saying that such research had already been carried on (which was not true), and the results might be damaging to the police (which was quite likely).

Problems of Selective Access

The second major limitation imposed by the present legal balance is the selective process by which researchers are denied or granted access to information. The survey of German researchers conducted at Bielefeld demonstrates that the success of a research project will often depend upon the status and connections of the principal researcher. To some extent, this question is related to the preceding discussion on the limitation of subject matter: if the researcher is polite and does not appear to be threatening, then he may be considered domesticated and granted entrance.

The problem of access is complicated by the fact that not every researcher is competent. Not everyone should be allowed access simply on the grounds of economy—there is a limit to how many researchers should be permitted to study an organization. A process of certification exists which tries to resolve these problems of status and competency, but it is informal and exercised on an ad hoc, case-by-case basis.

There are occasional governmental commissions in the federal government of the United States that have enormous access—they are not only well financed and have a large staff, but they even have the power to subpoena witnesses and records. Because of the prestige of the persons involved in the commission and the staff, they are more able to withstand pressure for suppression or manipulation by Congress or other groups.

In contrast, the role of the sociologist is much less exalted—especially in Germany, where the social sciences are not as fully developed. One German social scientist stated that sociologists have a much more difficult time in gaining access—especially to legal institutions—than lawyers: "Just the label 'sociologist' will make it impossible to do some types of research."

Generally, access is granted on the basis of private agreements with individual researchers. There are some advantages to the present informal certification procedure. Official discretion is not always found in a single unified body. Rather this discretion may be found in bureaucrats throughout the chain of command, and in some cases throughout several organizations. For example, in foreign policy there may be "leaks" from the State Department, the White House, the CIA, the Defense Department, or the Congress. The journalists have cultivated this system of information sources throughout the government. One advantage journalists have is their ability to publish information without citing sources. However, scholars are held to high standards of verification and documentation. Use of information that is not verified and not readily available to other researchers undermines the research process.

Because of these informal procedures, the state (and other bureaucracies) can pick and choose their interpreters. There is no rule of
law, just a bestowing of royal favor. Some researchers obtained
access in the past, others will be successful in the future. The serious
question is, Which individuals will be permitted access and why?
Hopefully, formal administrative procedures will be increasingly
utilized, including criteria for selection, a hearing, a written decision,
and judicial review.

Despite the limitations of the present system, there is a certain
advantage to disorganization and chaos—"There is a certain invigorat-
ing free-for-all in the United States where a significant amount of
information is obtained in an adversarial and unsystematic fashion."
Any proposed remedy should be carefully weighed to insure that the
cure is not worse than the current problems flowing from the royal
touch.

The Interests of the State

Government is the subject of research—and very rarely is it a
willing subject. It has a monopoly of information over many areas
such as foreign affairs or criminal justice. Perhaps the prime example
of government regulation of access to information is the classification system. Currently, information about foreign affairs in the
United States is classified from twenty-five to thirty years. Although
there may be a few areas where some secrecy is necessary, such as
weapon development or current international negotiations, the vast
bulk of information currently classified relates to policy formulation,
justifications for official action, and the nature of the official actions
themselves—matters that are not vital to the national security but
that are essential to an informed public review of state action.

The state has a strong tradition of secrecy—especially in Germany.
The government needs some degree of secrecy in order to function.
A recent example in Germany involved a case in which a civil servant
who was also a graduate student wrote a doctoral dissertation on
material that he collected in his capacity as a government official. His
superiors forbade him to publish the dissertation on the grounds that
it would injure the privacy of citizens who had given the information
to the government without the expectation that it would be used for
research. Another example from Germany concerned the unsuccessful attempt of researchers to obtain data about the recruitment
policies of the German foreign office, which refused to make
available any background data about its employees such as religion,
education, or previous jobs. To what extent does the state have an
obligation to protect the privacy of its citizens? How can this
obligation be distinguished from the naked suppression of informa-

tion that may merely be embarrassing to individual bureaucrats or to the state in general?

Concern about the privacy of citizens is justified, but protective measures may further shield government from outside inspection. For instance, a German statute prohibits officials from revealing information in government files. Although this statute allows government agencies to share information, outside researchers are not included. Another example is pending German federal legislation on data banks. Only certain types of information may be given to private citizens, and then only under very serious regulations.

In some instances, this secrecy shields illegal acts, whether it is Hitler's Third Reich or Nixon's presidency. Indeed, the persons who administer the state may be the major criminals in society. How can social science reveal and attempt to combat this type of governmental illegality unless it holds some power of its own?

In a more positive vein, the state needs research in order to survive and to give service to its citizens. The evaluation of government programs is essential if the state is to attempt to meet its goals. To the extent that researchers can demonstrate that they can assist the state in carrying out its functions, they will be granted greater access.

Social science will become increasingly important in our future society. In the past forty years, the physical sciences have been important and, as a result, have been manipulated by the state for its own purposes. This type of control is quite likely to be applied to the social sciences, in relatively subtle ways—the ordering of priorities, the favoring of certain disciplines or individual researchers, and attempts to direct methodology.

Government agencies are not merely passive consumers of research. They actively seek out proposals around different political themes. Hopefully, this activism can be useful in filling gaps in knowledge. But a heavy price is being paid. Half of the money that is spent by government goes to support the government research establishment. The more the government spends on soliciting, reviewing, and monitoring research, the less is available for actually performing research by persons outside the government.

The larger the governmental role in research, the greater the potential for government censorship through denial of funds. The political nature of research was exemplified recently in the United States when the Law Enforcement Assistance Administration terminated all behavioral modification programs. Although these programs had been lavishly encouraged during the preceding three years, they were summarily ended because of some adverse newspaper criticism.

Research conducted by or for government can have very serious negative consequences. For instance, in Nazi Germany (1933-45) there was an extreme centralization of research. The only function of scientific inquiry was to aid the Nazi regime. Not only were many persons harmed by the conduct of various types of research, especially medical experiments, but also whole areas of knowledge were subverted to meet the dictates of the state. As a result of this experience, the state constitution of Bremen has an express protection of citizens from research, even if it means that a specific project must be limited or completely prohibited.

In the United States, the government as a researcher has caused many of the most serious abuses in research. Two government projects in particular have resulted in a popular outcry—one involving syphilis experiments in the South and the other the sterilization of medical subjects. Now that the government has created this serious problem, the universities and nongovernment agencies are used as scapegoats and are being made to conform to heavy government regulation.

The state is acquiring its own research capacity. Almost every branch of government has its own research department—the primary purposes of which are to justify governmental programs, to be an apologist for the status quo, and to act as the gatekeeper for access by researchers outside government.

There is a growing serious problem of the relation of the few independent researchers to the government research establishment. Criminal-justice researchers in the United States may find it increasingly difficult to be independent of the Law Enforcement Assistance Administration as they serve on advisory committees, receive grants, work in the bureaucracy in Washington on visiting fellowships, etc. In Germany, almost all researchers are government civil servants, although they enjoy a special constitutionally protected status.

Despite the negative impact of the state, it also should have a serious interest in the freedom of research. As the representative of the people it has the final authority and responsibility for weighing the interests involved. For example, a statute in the German state of Hess requires researchers to consider the social consequences of their work.

But finally, and most important, the government is supposed to be the servant of its citizens. Too often it is the master. The free exchange of ideas and information about government is a right and necessity in a democratic society. Citizens in a democracy must make choices about their lives and about their government. They need research and information in order to make these choices. The government has no right of privacy except in very temporary or limited circumstances. There should at least be a presumption in favor of open government.

In conclusion, these are the alternatives which result from the current status of government regulation of access:

1. *Conduct no research at all.* This alternative would seriously undermine the democratic quality of our government and, indeed, make government difficult in our mass society.

2. *Rely on official channels.* This is time consuming and often highly selective. By relying on the granting of royal favor, the research process becomes captive to the established bureaucracies.

3. *Obtain documents illegally or get information from governmental "leaks."* Information obtained this way cannot be cited or made generally available. The whole process is subject to serious manipulation. At a minimum, researchers will need immunity from criminal or civil liability.

4. *Conduct confidential interviews with bureaucrats.* Here, the need for a testimonial privilege is paramount.

TESTIMONIAL PRIVILEGE

A testimonial privilege protects researchers from compulsory production of oral or documentary evidence in court or other tribunals. In the United States, the pertinent question about testimonial privileges is not whether the privileges should exist, but rather how they should be drafted. The United States Congress in 1970 gave an absolute protection to persons engaged in drug and alcohol research, but required registration with the Secretary of the Department of Health, Education and Welfare. A 1972 statute gave less protection (e.g., the judiciary would have to weigh the interest at stake in each case), but it did not require any registration. An amendment to the statute reinstituting the Law Enforcement Assistance Administration in 1973 gave broad protection to research information collected as a result of funding from that federal agency.

In addition, there is some protection for researchers under statutes and cases currently governing news media privileges. For example, Delaware expressly included researchers when it passed a newsmen-shield statute in 1973.

Arguably, researchers should have even *more* protection than newsmen. There is usually less motivation for a research subject to speak than the confidential informants of newsmen. Then, too, the law governing research is even less well defined than that concerned with news media. While some media leaders such as the CBS network or the *New York Times* are willing to pay the price of litigation, few researchers or even universities would be willing to take on the expenses of protracted test litigation that would benefit the profession as a whole. Finally, research projects take a longer time than most media stories. It is not unusual for a research project to last three or four years; so the researcher may have more to lose than a journalist.

Although German journalists enjoy a testimonial privilege, there was no suggestion that researchers would be protected in a similar fashion. The Germans did not see the researcher, as some Americans do, as a "slow journalist." Rather, they saw his function and method as fundamentally different from those of the researcher: "The journalist is merely someone who finds out facts and then publishes opinions about these facts. The researcher is much more scientific and professional. His job is much more difficult." In the United States, the two are seen as being much more closely related.

Three basic issues were raised about the nature of a testimonial privilege: (1) the definition of a "researcher"; (2) the role of confidentiality; and (3) the need for a showing of public benefit.

The Definition of a "Researcher"

It is difficult to define the word "researcher" for the purpose of protection. Any attempt should carefully weigh the merits of possible licensing by government or any other body (including professional associations) which might result from any attempt to bestow the advantage of a testimonial privilege on a definable group.

The speakers argued repeatedly against the creation of a central office, especially if it was run by the state, which would certify researchers. The power to certify is the power to regulate and censor the research community.

One alternative is not to make any definition in advance, but to leave this determination to a judge or jury to decide in each case. In Germany, the statute granting the privilege for journalists does not define the term. In this country, the Delaware statute that grants the testimonial privilege to researchers does not attempt to define who is a "researcher."

A related problem is attempting to state what research methods would be acceptable, i.e., defining the "researcher" by what he does. There was considerable objection to the idea of protecting only research data collected by "recognized" methods. Especially in Germany, where social science is less developed than the United States, this definition could be a very serious limiting factor on the growth of social-science methodology. Is participant-observer a recognized technique? Is data surveillance a recognized technique?

The answer to such questions may vary depending on the person asked or the particular application.

In general, however, the more absolute the protection granted, the narrower the definition must be. If an absolute protection not to testify is being granted, there will be strong pressure from society to define the recipients in narrow terms.

By giving the privilege to some, others will necessarily be excluded. The more exceptions to the protection that are made, the greater the opportunity to find that areas are not covered. Therefore, if a statutory privilege is to be created, it should be as broad or absolute as possible.

Another basic issue was whether to adopt a *status* approach (e.g., how many academic degrees does the person have?) or a *functional* approach (e.g., what is the person's activity?). The functional approach may be necessary in projects employing fairly large teams of workers with a variety of credentials and responsibilities. Interviewers or key-punch operators may be part of the research team, and they need the protection of being a "researcher" even though they may lack advanced university degrees or other formal criteria.

The Role of Confidentiality

On the one hand, protection might be predicated on the existence of a confidential relationship. Proponents of this view note that it is extremely difficult, perhaps impossible, to define a researcher without setting up a system of licensing. Instead of looking at the formal criteria of the researcher, this approach focuses on the protection of the privacy of the research subject. It would protect only those relationships where there was a promise of confidentiality.

Others would protect any research relationship, regardless of whether or not there was an expressed promise of confidentiality. Proponents here argue that a promise of confidentiality is impossible or meaningless in many areas of research. It would be impractical to obtain a promise of confidentiality in dealing with large groups, for instance. In many cases, participation in research projects is not voluntary (e.g., the study of persons receiving a guaranteed annual income). Some individuals, such as children or mental patients, cannot consent to be studied. Should the consent be required of parent or legal guardian, which, in cases of institutionalization, might be the state? Moreover, even if a promise is given, the research subject quickly forgets the researcher's presence, and may continue to commit illegal or embarrassing acts.

The expectations of subjects are that their information will only be used in a statistical or anonymous form. These expectations ought to be protected as a matter of status or statute; they cannot be protected merely by a contract between each researcher and his or her subject. (Perhaps there should be surveys to determine how much information can be given with or without a promise of confidentiality.)

One problem is that the psychologists have misled so many people in the course of their experiments that the notion of informed consent has become debased throughout social science. Now, no one can believe what is told him in a research situation.

Ethnographic studies are another area that need protection but in which it is impossible to give a pledge of confidentiality. Examples include Laud Humphrey's study of homosexual activity in public places or Jonathan Rubenstein's study of the police in Philadelphia. In both cases, the researcher participated in the activity being studied—Humphrey by being a lookout for homosexuals in public washrooms and Rubenstein by joining the Philadelphia police force.

Another type of research in which a pledge of confidentiality is not possible is the use of administrative records or data surveillance. Two examples come from the experience of sociologist Marvin Wolfgang. In one, he collected data about a birth cohort of 10,000 boys born in Philadelphia in 1945. Their careers were studied by compiling records from schools, police, and selective service. In compiling this information, a new type of information is created that needs protection. In the second study, concerning the application of the death penalty, public information of about 3000 rape cases in the South was studied to determine whether there was any racial differential in sentencing. The researchers received the consent of neither the criminal nor the victim. Most of the information was obtained by secondary data, although occasionally there were interviews by field researchers. In any event, the synthesized data created a unique set of information.

One solution to the confidentiality problem might be suggested by a draft of the Uniform Newsmen Privilege Statute which makes a distinction between the protection afforded confidential and non-confidential information. Under this proposed model statute, the journalist's work product which was not confidential would be protected only as part of a balancing of the interests involved, while confidential information would be absolutely protected.

The Need for a Showing of Public Benefit

There was general opposition to an *expressed* requirement that, in order to be protected, the research should have public benefit. An expressed requirement of "public benefit" could be as harmful as exceptions to the free flow of information like the "national security"; such exceptions are so vague that they may become all encompassing. Also, the benefit of research is often difficult to demonstrate. It may be many decades before the true benefit is seen. In a sense, only research projects that have already been completed and the results demonstrated can show any benefits. However, almost everyone realized that, in order to receive a special status, researchers must demonstrate that their work has some potential value or social utility—whether or not an expressed showing of "public benefit" is required.

The rationale for including the term "public benefit" was an attempt to exclude from protection research done solely for private benefit, such as most important consultation which is not published. If the purpose of a "public benefit" requirement is to exclude private and nonpublished research, this limitation on coverage should be written into the statute in those terms.

Possible Abuses of Testimonial Privilege

Two major problems were raised—the use of government undercover agents and remedies for the corrupt, dishonest, or merely sloppy researcher.

Could a general testimonial privilege be abused by undercover police agents? By statute, the subjects could be given the power to consent to waiving the privilege—which they could not do if "the researcher" was really a police agent. In Germany the answer would in part be governed by paragraph 54 of the Penal Procedural Code, which prohibits police agents from testifying without the permission of their superiors. In the United States, undercover agents could be barred as a matter of policy from testifying without the permission of their superiors.

The problem of the corrupt, unethical, or sloppy researcher might be met in four ways. (1) The social-science profession itself must begin to discipline and regulate its members. Most of the American social scientists felt that there would be no meaningful self-regulation by the social-science associations. However, if social scientists want special privileges such as testimonial privilege, they will have to police their own ranks. Lawyers and doctors have testimonial privileges, but these professions also disbar corrupt or unethical members of the profession. (2) The waiver provisions of the statute could give the privilege to both the subject and the researcher. There is a need for the research subject to have some power in regulating the relationship and thus protect himself. (3) There is a possible remedy of libel action. Although in the United States public figures such as government officials have little chance of recovery (*New York Times v. Sullivan*), there is a growing possibility that "non-public" persons may be able to collect for libel. (4) Penalties could be provided in the statute to safeguard against unwarranted disclosure of identity. These penalties might include treble damages, but injunctions would probably not be possible because of the prior restraint aspects of the First Amendment.

IMMUNITY FROM CRIMINAL AND CIVIL LIABILITY

Research about crime constantly raises questions about the liability or responsibility of researchers. In particular, it is difficult to study aggression in society and at the same time exclude the problem that some of the subjects may commit or receive bodily injury.

A precedent for immunity is the German federal law which provides that the transfer of forbidden drugs is not punished if it is research licensed by the government. Similar immunities exist in the United States for research in drugs.

Two important conditions must be noted for any requests of immunity. First, this must be the only way to gather the data, i.e., all other research avenues have been tested and found wanting. Second, the method that injures society or individuals least must be selected.

The following examples of possible criminal or civil liability suggest the range of problems.

1. A researcher interviews prostitutes about their life style, knowing that they are going to break the law in a few minutes by soliciting cutomers.

2. A researcher knows that a burglar is about to commit a crime. Does he have an obligation to tell the police? Does he become an accessory to crime?

3. A researcher in interviewing a heroin addict learns that the subject has a $50-a-day habit and that he gets this money from robbery. He has a female accomplice stand on a street corner pretending to be a prostitute. When a perspective customer takes her to the entrance of an apartment, the criminal robs the victim at the point of a knife. (If the researcher knew exactly when the robbery was going to take place, he might have more of an obligation to report the crime to the police.)

4. A convicted criminal is currently on a work-release program from prison. One day he refuses to return to the prison. He goes to the researcher and demands money and a place to stay, saying that, if he does not receive them, he will commit robbery to get the money. Does it make a difference if the researcher's intention in complying

with the request is to convince the prisoner to return to the institution?

5. A researcher wants to study a large insurance corporation, in particular its hiring and termination procedures. He is refused permission to study the organization as a researcher. Instead, he obtains a job as a doorman and messenger in the company. He uses this position to gather information and make observations. He could only get the job by using a false identity card, because he was already known in his true identity by the corporation and would not have been hired.

6. A researcher is attempting to study the status of foreign workers in German companies. He gains access by using a false identity and forged passport.

7. A researcher is a participant-observer in a youth gang which gets involved in a street fight. He retreats with the gang after the fight, leaving an injured member of the rival gang in the street calling for help. (This is especially a problem under German law, which places an affirmative obligation on a stranger to assist an injured person.)

The need for immunity is probably greater where the researcher is studying the higher levels of the social order. Among the rich and powerful, the consequence of betraying secrets and revealing information is often more serious than studying the lower strata of society. The harassment of Ralph Nader by General Motors during his study of the automotive industry is one example of bureaucratic power. At the higher orders of society, there is greater likelihood that researchers will be criminally prosecuted or that they or their subjects will lose their jobs.

As a practical matter, it may be politically difficult to get immunity. The best solution is to increase access. The relationship to access is highlighted by the attempt by the Nixon administration to amend the espionage acts to make it a crime not only to *give* classified information but also for the journalist or researcher to *receive* the information. The Pentagon Papers investigation and the Popkin case are dramatic examples of the bureaucracy attempting to plug the leaks and keep the public ignorant or informed only by "official" sources.

Even if the researcher illegally gains access, there are serious limitations on his ability to gather information because of his concealed status. Like an international spy, the researcher working in disguise can only ask certain questions and have access to certain documents without revealing his true identity. He is not free to ask a set of systematic questions. Instead, he must play his role in the organization.

Possible courses of action that might ameliorate the problems of criminal and civil liability include:

1. The use by the researcher of the privilege against self-incrimination.

2. The criminal law—which already punishes too much—should be rewritten. For example, in the United States the crime of misprision of felony purports to punish the failure to report crime. However, the statute is never enforced and should be abolished.

3. Immunity might be given for minor crimes and a study made of the effects on the research process and on law enforcement.

4. Researchers should work closely with journalists who have developed techniques and sources for collecting data. The researcher has the advantage of having more time. He is fitting together pieces of information in a mosaic over a period of time. Little cooperation to date has been developed between the two professions, either collectively or on an individual basis.

5. Researchers should turn the occasional prosecution or lawsuit to their advantage. The inconvenience and monetary loss is part of the cost of being researchers. Their ultimate objective is to gain publicity for their results and to affect public policy. Instead of being a burden, prosecution or legal action should be turned into a benefit by taking advantage of the publicity potential.

Any decision to grant immunity will require a weighing of the public benefit from research against the injury to others. A scale of seriousness is useful. For serious crimes such as murder, there should be a legal and moral obligation to report the crime and to make sure that there is no injury. The minimum condition in granting immunity is that there should be no physical harm to people as a result of the research.

On the other hand there are minor crimes, perhaps gambling or prostitution, in which persons are not usually injured and the researcher might more readily gain immunity.

There is a middle ground between the serious crimes involving physical harm and the relatively harmless ones. Cases falling in this middle ground would have to be decided on their facts. For example, the failure to aid an injured person must be weighed against such factors as the seriousness of his injury and the likelihood that others will assist him.

Although everyone agreed that no physical harm should result because of the research, the argument was made that there are hundreds of cases each year where someone fails to aid a person injured in the street, and almost no one is prosecuted for that failure. The one or two cases in which a researcher is involved will mean very little in terms of the persons actually injured, but the work of the researcher may help solve the serious underlying social problem.

In response, it was argued that physical harm should not be permitted under any circumstances. What record of success have social scientists shown that they should be allowed an immunity from the normal obligations of citizenship? It is impossible to say that a few must suffer now to help many later on.

These positions were highlighted in the following exchange between a constitutional lawyer and a social scientist, both of them German: *Photocopy.*

Constitutional lawyer: The researcher should not be given an immunity from the criminal laws. There are almost always other ways of researching the problem. If there is no other way but to cause or allow harm to be done to others, then let us accept as a fact that certain fields cannot be investigated. There must be some limits to research.

On the one hand of the balance we have the proposition that in the distant future there is a hope of changing an important social problem such as fighting crime by learning more about it. On the other hand, we have the very immediate problem of a person who may bleed to death because he is not given assistance.

This type of problem is reminiscent of the research conducted in Nazi Germany in world War II where people were frozen to death or subjected to other inhumane treatment in the name of science. Perhaps some people eventually benefited from this research, but it is now universally criticized.

You must show to me the difference between any proposed immunity from criminal prosecution and the Hitler scientist. Otherwise, this immunity from prosecution can not be justified.

Social scientist: The researcher in leaving the scene of the street fight is not damaging anyone. He did not participate in the criminal activity. He did not pick up a club and strike someone. The only question is whether possibly his presence gives emotional assistance to the street fighters or possibly that his failure to report the crime would lead to bodily injury.

Constitutional lawyer: The Nazi scientist was not hitting anyone. He was merely sitting and watching someone die of cold temperatures, while he recorded the experiment. To that extent at least, the researcher was assisting in the infliction of pain and injury to a fellow human being. He did not fight against this system; he did not try to help a person who is dying.

A final problem about immunity: Should the researcher receive immunity from *all* crimes, not just the crime which he may view or participate in during his research? The need for this broad immunity is that government can always find a handle to punish the researcher for crimes unrelated to his profession such as tax violations. Such universal immunity would be impossible to grant, but the problem highlights the vulnerability of the researcher and the ability of the establishment and government to harass and silence its critics.

THE CONSTITUTIONAL, LEGAL, AND ETHICAL BASIS FOR PROTECTION

In the United States and in Germany there are several constitutional provisions or theories that would support special treatment of researchers such as a testimonial privilege or criminal immunity.

In the United States, the major bases are as follows: (1) The First Amendment, which mandates a free flow of information. (2) The research subject's right of privacy. *Cf. Griswold v. Connecticut* (statute regulating the sale of contraceptives unconstitutionally violates right of privacy). (3) The "necessary and proper" clause, which protects essential government functions, would be especially useful in protecting the evaluation of federal and state programs. (4) The commerce clause has been suggested as a basis for federal protection of the news media, and might be useful in providing the basis for a federal statute in the research area.

Pertinent provisions of the German constitution include:

1. Section 5, Article 3 of the West German federal constitution expressly protects the freedom of research, but the effect is doubtful. However, there is a decision originating from the state of Lower Saxony in which a state statute was declared unconstitutional because it gave nonresearchers the right to participate and help determine research policy to the extent that the ultimate policy-making authority had been taken away from the researchers. The German constitutional court found that this violated the constitutional freedom of research. Opinion about this provision has been split between those who believe that it confers a positive right on the researcher to obtain access to information and those who say that it merely confers a negative protection from governmental censorship or interference. Since there has been little attempt by the government to interfere directly with or censor research, there has been little need under this latter approach to invoke this section since its adoption in 1948.

2. The right to practice a profession is also protected by the German federal constitution. The argument based on this section is that the state pays the researcher to collect information. The state gives researchers this responsibility, and it cannot forbid them to engage in their profession, which is predicated on having access to certain types of information. An analogy would be made to the

judge, who requires certain independence and objectivity. This is part of the judicial function; it is not merely a privilege. Similarly, the researcher must have independence and access to carry out his profession. Use of the freedom of professions as a basis for protecting researchers has been criticized because this approach would require further legislation, which could lead to licensing by the state.

3. The right of institutions to conduct research is similar to the right of academic freedom in the United States. There is a need for certain organizations (e.g., universities) to be autonomous and independent, if they are to carry on the search for knowledge. The case from Lower Saxony striking down a state statute which gave a deciding role in relation to nonresearch personnel on research governing bodies is an example of an application of the guarantee of institutional freedom.

4. The right of privacy and freedom of the arts are other relevant provisions.

Each of the foregoing constitutional protections must be balanced with countervailing factors such as the obligation of each citizen to give his evidence in a civil and criminal trial (e.g., the Sixth Amendment, which guarantees the right of criminal defendants to call witnesses and to confront witnesses called against them). Other conflicting demands include the duty to report crime, the obligation to help an injured person, and the protection of citizens from libel and slander.

Although in both Germany and the United States there may be some interference with the research process, does the problem rise to the level of constitutional importance? The United States Constitution speaks only in general terms about the right of freedom of expression. There must be a showing that the interferences are serious and that, for example, the loss of confidential sources without the creation of a testimonial privilege will be so serious that the whole research process is jeopardized.

A judgment about the present situation in both countries is largely subjective. There are no allegations that the government is actively suppressing information or burning books. The government is simply not assisting researchers in obtaining some kinds of information. It is probably not enough that one or two projects are put in jeopardy.

Consequently, almost no one would argue that research has a constitutional right to an *absolute* protection against the dictates of other considerations. The constitutional rights in both countries (e.g., research in Germany and freedom of expression in the United States) must be weighed against other factors.

Who should do this weighing? Should it be the judges on a

case-by-case basis? A problem with the present ad hoc, case-by-case decision is that researchers at the moment lack ground rules. It is difficult to determine what researchers and methods will be protected.

The most complete type of protection could be given by a constitutional provision that gave *researchers* an absolute protection in every case. It is hard to imagine researchers being given this power by society.

The next alternative would be giving the power to the legislature, the most democratic body in society. Legislation would have the advantage of establishing certain basic ground rules with individual determinations being made by the judiciary. Legislation would give more validity to any claim made by an individual researcher. As more government money becomes available to researchers and they attempt to probe the more sensitive areas in society, there will be an increasing need for legislators to define the proper boundaries.

Barring very specific statutory regulation, the courts will be called upon to weigh the merits of each case. The courts will develop a common-law understanding of what can and cannot be done by researchers.

In the United States, some prosecutors have accepted self-limitation and regulation in this area. The Department of Justice was a leader when it issued guidelines for subpoenas to journalists in protecting confidential sources of information. These guidelines have largely resolved the question at the federal level by granting a large degree of freedom to newsmen. Similar protection from federal prosecutorial subpoenas could be granted to researchers.

Finally, there was the recurring suggestion that a research committee based in a university or research organization have broad powers to confer testimonial privilege and perhaps even immunity from criminal and civil laws. In the United States, this would require an extension of the committees presently existing under the general supervision of the Department of Health, Education and Welfare which call for the peer group review of medical research. Under the proposed expansion, the legislature would set broad guidelines for the conduct of social-science research, and the research review committees would operate as administrative agencies, with the courts insuring due process and resolving specific disputes.

Regardless of the constitutional and legal consequences of the researcher's actions, ethical problems are also presented. Two examples give some suggestion of the ethical consideration:

1. A social scientist was a participant-observer of the gypsies in Austria in 1941-42. In studying this group and living with them, he

witnessed many criminal acts. He had never told them that he was a researcher. His dilemma about publishing his results was resolved when he was imprisoned by the Nazi regime. One of his co-workers hid the information he had collected which was published after World War II.

2. In the United States, researchers working on the National Commission on Violence, as part of an attempt to develop counter-measures to political assassination, prepared a systems analysis on how to murder the president of the United States. After the study had served its purpose it was destroyed. The researchers decided that any value in making this manual generally available was outweighed by the obvious dangers inherent in its publication.

In neither the case of the Austrian gypsies nor the study of how to assassinate the U.S. president was any law broken. However, in both cases the researchers felt a moral or ethical restraint; that they should not encourage the repression of an ethnic group on the one hand, or the murder of the president of the country on the other.

Other questions were raised by the alleged neutrality of research-ers. Are they merely like a videotape machine which records what is happening, or do they have an effect upon the behavior they are witnessing (e.g., could the mere presence of a researcher encourage his subjects to commit an illegal act?)?

At least two approaches to the ethical problems were mentioned. On the one hand, it was felt that this was a matter for individual situational ethics. The researcher must decide largely for himself, based on the circumstances of a given moment, how he shall respond.

On the other hand, it was argued that situational ethics could lead to cultural relativism in which "anything goes." According to this view, situational ethics plays into the hands of bureaucrats who are only interested in maintaining the status quo. Instead, there is a need to develop transnational or transcendental ethics.

The key question was, To whom does the researcher owe alliance? Is it to the current system, in particular the nation-state, or is it to some system of values that transcends national boundaries? This school of thought was reminiscent of the eighteenth-century Enlight-enment, where an international community of scholars and an independent set of values sought to transcend the values and goals of the reigning monarch.

CONCLUSION, AND A POSSIBLE SOLUTION

Any attempt to simplify a discussion as varied and rich as occurred during the three days at Bielefeld should be undertaken with caution.

However, it seemed that there were two major strains of discussion—one conservative, the other interventionist.

The conservatives were largely content with the status quo and would not seek any serious changes in the balance of power between researchers and government. They argued that it is not possible to study everything; there must be some limits to knowledge. The granting of special privileges and immunities to researchers will create a special elitist category that is not justified by its function. There is no moral claim to complete freedom. Much of the sentiment for preserving the status quo was based on a fear that the reforms might be worse than the present set of problems, for example that a testimonial privilege would lead to government licensing and regulation of researchers.

According to the conservatives, the decision to grant any special status to the research process lies with society, which must weigh the merit gained from the research process against the possible injury or harm resulting. Although society may choose to set general guidelines acting through the legislature, the process is probably best left to a case-by-case determination where judges can weigh the facts and equities presented in each case.

In contrast to the conservatives, the interventionists (generally those conducting empirical research) wanted to change the present balance between researcher and bureaucracy.

The most important victory already won by proponents of this point of view is the Freedom of Information Act adopted by the U.S. Congress in 1966. This statute puts the burden on the government to prove why information must be withheld from the public domain. Although the exceptions to the act, such as national security, provide severe limitations, its power is significant.

According to the interventionists, access is granted as a natural condition in the natural sciences, but the social scientist is everywhere restricted. The researcher needs protection from government and private retaliation. Any research has political consequences. Karl Marx would now be regarded as a serious researcher, but a hundred years ago he would have been classified as a dangerous opponent of the state. The research of a political scientist about the government will be seen as oppositional politics. Research is increasingly empirical and increasingly will have collisions with existing bureaucracies. The whole notion of action research makes it impossible to separate research from politics. A researcher comments about government and other broad social policies. It is impossible to separate research from the process of political participation.

Case-by-case determination, especially by judges, is not an adequate safeguard. There is a need for stability and planning and firm guidelines that will not come from individual cases. Also, judges will be largely in favor of the establishment and status quo, and will not properly balance the interests of researchers. The interventionists argue that absolute protections of information sources and immunity are necessary.

The conservative would emphasize the social obligation of the researcher to others. The researcher must worry about the impact of the publication on the subjects of the research. Ultimately, only the state can protect its citizens. In addition, there is a right of reanalysis and obligation to throw open the *researcher's data* to outside view.

In contrast, many empirical researchers argued that only the researcher can decide when and what he will reveal. "The researcher has certain rights and obligations; no one can weigh these for him in the first instance." The essence of freedom of research is for the researcher himself to determine what he says and does not say.

The conservative position argues that the researcher must bear certain risks as part of the price he must pay for freedom of his intellectual inquiry. In the past, researchers have been burned at the stake or expelled from the community. The researcher must have the courage of his convictions and believe in the importance of what he is doing. The lack of protection of confidential information and the possibility of criminal liability can be seen as positive factors. They raise important issues, and the researcher should from time to time worry about these questions. It takes courage to be a researcher.

The interventionists argue that normal people, not just supermen, should be able to conduct research. Researchers should not constantly be asked to put their reputations, livelihoods, and even their lives in jeopardy. The researcher should not have to take all the risks himself. He is performing an important social function, and he should receive some protection.

The conservative-interventionist debate was perhaps most clearly highlighted by the distinction in German law surrounding the constitutional protection of research. The conservative view is that this is merely a negative status which shields or protects existing social science. It guarantees that the state will not interfere with research. Based on this negative status, there have been few problems since 1945, since there have been few or no attempts of direct censorship. In contrast, the interventionists argue that there is a positive side to the constitutional protection of research; an obligation of the state to provide access to researchers.

One possible way of resolving this dichotomy was suggested—the creation of review panels. These panels would be similar to or part of the peer-group review panels existing now in the United States for medical research. The emphasis would be on the protection of the research process and the certification of specific research projects, rather than individual researchers.

Under the present system, the researcher must bear all of the responsibility. Any determination about whether or not the research-er acted legally or ethically is now determined at the end of the project—generally when it is too late for the researcher to do anything about it. The review panels provide a mechanism for the researcher to learn before he starts his research.

Anyone could engage in research; but, in order to obtain research privileges such as immunity or testimonial privilege, the research project would have to be done under the protection of a research institution. All of the power of decision cannot be given to the researcher who is too close to his own project and lacks neutrality and impartiality. On the other hand, it is dangerous to give this power to the state to certify and license research projects. Rather, a broad-based review of the research design and its implementation could be made by fellow researchers. Scientists would be in a better position than judges to determine proper methodology or to weigh the benefits to be obtained by the research in each project.

The review panel should contain not only scientists but also representatives of the communities being studied, and could also include persons from the research bureaucracy. The review board should be approved by the government, but not controlled by it.

In West Germany, these boards could be incorporated into university constitutions which establish interdisciplinary agencies to define the research projects and the nature of the research process itself.

There were arguments against giving such power to review panels. The panels might inhibit the development of new methodologies or subjects. The present free-for-all, unregulated approach, although it places stress and responsibilities on the individual researcher, still provides a fair amount of freedom.

 *Chapter Two*

Ethical Issues of Research in Criminology

Marvin Wolfgang

The variety of situations in which criminological scholars might be immune from prosecution has been explored by other contributors.[1] I wish to lay out only one kind of instance as an example of the dangers to which the Center for Studies in Criminology and Criminal Law at the University of Pennsylvania could be exposed. The example demonstrates several principles, and therefore is transferable and less parochial than at first it may seem.

Delinquency in a Birth Cohort, published by the University of Chicago Press in 1972, was a study of approximately 10,000 boys born in 1945 who lived in Philadelphia from ages 10 to 18.[2] There were no ethical problems in that data collection and analysis, for we had complete cooperation from the Board of Education, the Archdiocese, and private schools with regard to access to school records. Moreover, the Philadelphia Police Department and Selective Service granted us permission to compare names and birthdates in order to determine which boys who registered for selective service had a delinquency record. Our analyses of those data are fully recorded in the book.

In 1970 we obtained a research grant from the National Institute of Mental Health (NIMH) to study a 10-percent sample of the birth cohort and to interview as many members we could locate. After very diligent investigative work we located approximately 60 percent of the sample and asked them questions that required interviews of an hour or more. None whom we found refused to be interviewed. We had no "informed consent" form in those days. We asked many questions concerning their student, occupational, marital, military, and gang memberships, and other personal histories.

But the items that were of special interest to us for analysis of their histories up to age 26 were self-reportings of delinquencies prior to age 18 and crimes committed from ages 18 to 26. We asked if they had committed any of the following offenses before and after age 18:

Table 2-1.   Offenses Committed Before and After Age 18

1. Been out past curfew
2. Played hookey from school
3. Run away from home
4. Made an obscene phone call
5. Hurt someone badly enough to require medical treatment
6. Used heroin
7. Taken a car for joyriding
8. Disturbed the people in a neighborhood with loud noises
9. Set off a fire alarm for the fun of it
10. Threatened to hurt someone if he didn't give money or something else
11. Taken some money from someone without his knowing it
12. Had heroin in your possession
13. Smoke pot
14. Stolen something from a store
15. Passed a bad check
16. Forced a female to have sexual intercourse with you
17. Broken into a residence, store, school, or other enclosed area
18. Used a weapon to threaten another person
19. Helped a girl to have an abortion
20. Purposely damaged or destroyed property
21. Gone to a house of prostitution
22. Killed someone not accidentally
23. Been drunk in public
24. Carried a gun without a permit
25. Carried a switch-blade or other big knife
26. Had pot in your possession
27. Hurt someone in a minor way, like knocking him down
28. Bought or accepted property which you knew was stolen
29. Had sexual intercourse before you were married
30. Had sex relations with another male

We also asked if they had been victimized by any offenses, whether the crimes they committed had resulted in their being arrested, and many other things.

For the purposes of this essay, the important point is that many of the young men revealed to our interviewers that they had committed a variety of crimes. This is not the first time such a self-report study had been conducted. The history of "hidden delinquency" studies is well recorded.[3] But most previous studies in the United States have been conducted with junior and senior high-school students who reported in mostly anonymous questionnaires or protected interviews relatively trivial and innocuous juvenile status offenses, like stealing from their mothers' pocketbooks, being truant, or committing petty larceny. Even the relatively sophisticated studies in Denmark, Norway, and Sweden dealt mostly with petty offenses. Self-reporting studies of crime and delinquency are known for their modest and relatively innocuous use of minor offenses. The birth cohort follow-up in Philadelphia sought to explore a much wider range of criminal offense behavior, including petty but also very serious crimes like robbery, burglary, rape, and even criminal homicide.

Four respondents informed us that they had been involved in criminal homicide—one before reaching 18—and 75 respondents claimed to have committed forcible rapes. The other offenses admitted are of less serious character but may still be viewed as important by police agencies. It is important to note that these are acts for which none of the respondents had ever been arrested.

There are several major ethical, scientific, and legal issues involved in the collection of these data:

1. *To what extent are the responses valid?*

There is considerable literature on this question ever since the early Short and Nye[4] studies of hidden delinquency. Robert Hardt[5] and more recently Martin Gold[6] have, among others, explored the topic and various ways to determine validity. Through interviews, after questionnaires, and through police-record checks of offenses for which respondents claimed to have been arrested, reasonable validity has been established. Austin Porterfield[7] once had a murder admitted for which there was no arrest in a set of offenses administered to university students. Our cohort population includes known offenders, a group that may be expected to have serious offenses in their unrecorded criminal histories.

2. *Should we have had written informed consent?*

Each cohort member who was located for an interview cooperated in general. Each was informed orally that the information would be kept strictly confidential, used only for research purposes, and analyzed in the aggregate, with no single individual identified or identifiable in the final research report. His cooperation in replying to questions, many of which were personal and sensitive, was obviously interpreted as his willingness to consent to the uses we announced at the outset. The interviews were conducted during 1971, which was a period just prior to the intensive concern for research with or on human subjects, prior to the requirement of the Department of Health, Education and Welfare that research proposals contain forms about such research, before university committees on research ethics were established, and before screening committees at HEW were functioning formally. Statutes, ordinances, and administrative regulations about privacy, informed consent, confidentiality, and accessibility to records were not yet devised or operating. In retrospect, it might be said that written consent should have been requested. But still, there are sound reasons against it.

Consider the psychology of the interview. The cohort subjects were generally contacted first by mail or telephone, but sometimes were directly approached at their front doors. Had a written consent been asked for, the young man might have wished to know more fully what he was consenting to. He could have asked to see the interview schedule, and thus the virtues and advantages of moving gradually from neutral to sensitive questions would have been lost. We cannot know how many refusals such a process would have promoted.

Moreover, the form of the written consent could or could not have contained reference to the refusal of the research staff to reveal information to the police or other authorities of the criminal justice system. Without such a reference, the form would have been inadequate and incomplete and therefore misleading. With the reference, without admitting that one or more of these agencies might have the authority to confiscate, or impound, our records, again it would have been incomplete and misleading. If the form admitted that our records could be impounded in the future, we would virtually have recruited refusals in such abundance that the project would have been aborted at the beginning. Besides, we did not know then and still do not know whether a court order could indeed impound the records, whether any member of the staff who had access to specific information could suffer prosecution and imprisonment for protecting records, or whether any effort to conceal data would be successful. In short, any written-consent form would have been misleading or would have promoted a series of additional questions, the answers to which our interviewers did not possess. Either lies or agnostic replies would have been the interviewers' responses to a variety of hypothetical questions. If the former, then unethical; if the latter, then nearly invited refusals to be interviewed could be expected.

The oral request for cooperation in a sociological research maintained a minimum of formality in the interaction between subject and interviewer, permitted the respondent to refuse answering any specific question along the way (of course, a written consent does not preclude specific question refusals), and permitted employment of the pretested positioning of sets of questions in order to maximize the likelihood of response. Announcing that the information would be used confidentially by the research staff was the maximum claim and the only intended use. The oral claim implied nothing more, the respondent inferred nothing less. The result was rapport and cooperation.

3. *Should the results of these interviews be published?*

In view of the events that have transpired about record-keeping and ethical issues in research on human subjects between the interviews and the present, this is a reasonable question.[8] Our Center gives an unequivocal affirmative. Publishing the results will be done with the protections announced in our letters and by the interviewers. No single individual will be identified or identifiable; all data will be aggregated, not only to maintain confidentiality but to provide for scientific statistical analyses as well.

However, it cannot be denied that publication in professional journals or books produces a new layer of visibility of the research. Newspapers and other media summarized our earlier original birth cohort study, thereby making the police and courts aware of the character of the study. The same will occur, I am sure, with publication of the follow-up that will report not only many of the personal, sociopsychological variables in the lives of the criminal and noncriminal cohort members, but also the self-reported delinquencies and crimes. At that point the research team[9] at the Center could be subject to pressure by the police and other agencies to reveal the names of those cohort members who informed us of their crimes. The danger of publication would then become a function of the degree to which threats of such pressure are real.

We still intend to publish, under the assumptions that (1) the threat is an unlikely event, and (2) our Center can effectively function as a buffer between our research subjects and the acquisition of our files by outside persons. These assumptions raise other questions that will be entertained later in this chapter. It should also be noted that the very publication of this chapter moves many of these issues to a higher visibility than does the quiet conduct of data analysis.

4. *Are members of the research staff accessories after the fact?*

Having obtained information about criminal offenses from specific, known, and identified subjects of a research project, the researchers stand in a posture a harboring information, if not hiding individuals or abetting escape. We do not have the mantle of the clergy or of medical practitioners to protect us, although the degree to which privileged information can be closeted in the minds of these professionals is in doubt, and courts have been known to request psychiatrists and psychologists to reveal such information. Probably the "crime," if any here, is misprision of a felony, which is obsolete in most jurisdictions but still an offense under federal law.

The traditional research response to the question is that the researcher is a neutral, disinterested recipient of data collected only for scientific research purposes. Information was sought and purposefully obtained to aid the scholarly enterprise, the intellectual pursuit, or even to provide guidance for a rational social policy. Data obtained that could have direct untoward consequences to subjects are not the possession of the state but of science. The research was not designed to treat, help, or harm individual subjects. The social scientist is not a representative of any branch of government with an obligation to execute certain police or judicial duties. It may be argued that technically he *is*, but the social definers do not perceive or define him as such. The scientist might contend that he is not even sure that the information given him is valid or correct; the rebuttal could be that it gives cause for official investigation.

5. *Are members of the research staff obstructing justice?*

This question is related to the previous one about being accessories, although they are questions about separate offenses. Even if the researcher is not deemed an accessory, even if satisfactorily precise definitions of "research" and "researcher" were presented to distinguish these terms[10] and roles from "journalist" and other fact-finders, a question about the obstruction of justice could still be raised in some quarters. To the extent that notions of justice are related to the punishment of offenders, anyone who has information about crimes committed by others (let alone oneself) is denying the system of justice its capacity to function relative to those offenders and those crimes. This crime, however, is generally construed in a much more narrow way, and usually requires obstruction of proceedings actually pending, with specific intent to do so.

Failure or unwillingness to report must be interpreted as placing a higher value on some other condition, in this case the conditions of scientific research that explicitly provide for confidentiality. The scientist responds again by asserting that were it not for his scientific pursuit, the information would not be available to authorities anyway, and that the research neither helps nor hinders the police and prosecutory functions of society so far as offense knowledge is concerned.

6. *Is there, nonetheless, an obligation to society and criminal justice to report this knowledge, an obligation that transcends the ethics of confidentiality or the interests of science?*

Putting aside questions of legality, this question asks whether the scientific researcher has broader moral responsibilities than his research perimeters. Given also the fact that no written informed consent was obtained, could revelation of criminal behavior by respondents be done with less impropriety, or would revelation be a worse ethical violation than not revealing the information? By some observers, the scientist may be viewed as ethically confined to his own myopia. He may be an analogue to the Defense Department bureaucrat who will not reveal to the larger society the Pentagon Papers of his own investigations. Yet there are clearly differences.

The scientist qua scientist is enveloped by the codes of conduct that his profession has created over a long history and with deep traditions. In the case under discussion he puts the value of protecting the individual whom he has sought and used for his research purposes above the interests of capture for criminal justice. Society until now has generally permitted the scientist his priority allocation. What we have said earlier is applicable here also; namely, that the scientist seems neither to help nor harm the individual respondent per se, nor to help nor hinder the criminal-justice system. His role is neither benign nor malevolent.

If a medical laboratory research project unrelated to cancer research inadvertently discovered that a volunteer subject had cancer, the researcher might feel rightly obligated to inform the subject, because such information might save a diseased person's life. Many other examples can be imagined in which revelations to the research subject and to others could have beneficial effects. Is it conceivable that a piece of information about a research subject may be discovered that would be harmful to him but of considerable benefit to many others? If so, no such situations exist in the criminological research we have been discussing. It may be said that if any researcher, a priori, has doubts about a moral obligation to violate the rubrics of confidentiality, he should absent himself from involvement in this kind of research. He would thereby satisfy his sense of ethics that lie outside the framework of those of science, as I have discussed them.

7. *What should a research center do if the police, prosecutor, or court requests the files?*

Our position is clear: we would not honor the request. We would make every effort, short of using aggressive force, to prevent the files from being examined or taken from the Center's premises. We would, if necessary, enter into litigation to protect the confidentiality of the records. There is no U.S. Supreme Court case we know of that affirms or rejects this position of members of the scientific research community. Unless or until such supreme declaration is made, we will stand firm in opposing any attempt to interfere with or intervene on our research territory. What we would do if the Supreme Court ordered our files to be opened to police or prosecutor is difficult to determine, but perhaps some answer appears in the comments that follow.

8. *Is the research staff immune from prosecution for contempt?*

If the staff is not viewed as accessory after the fact nor as obstructing justice, there is still the possibility that they may be held in contempt by a court if they do not submit the files to examination or impounding by a court order. Whether a research staff is immune from contempt is yet a matter to be determined by court testing. Lewis Yablonsky in California was requested, in a research on drug transfers, to testify about the persons involved, and he refused to divulge names. So far as I know, no further testing of his immunity was made, and no other test case of researcher immunity has appeared in the United States.

Were our Center's staff declared by the courts as not immune from prosecution, we would still maintain a posture of unwillingness to reveal names. Under this condition, we would seek litigation, as indicated in response to issue 7 above.

9. *Can a research staff develop a technique that can provide a fail-safe protection against identification of individual subjects in a research file?*

There is no definite answer. But there are techniques that surely would delay, if not forever prevent, such identification. One method is to have computer tapes on cards that have only identification numbers representing names for the file that is to be analyzed statistically in the aggregate. This suggestion was made by Alfred Blumstein for government files in *Science and Technology*, a Task Force Report for the President's Crime Commission.[11] Equivalent number-name combinations can be just a separate computer tape which can be deposited in a bank account in a foreign country where accounts are secretive. It is clear, however, that this process would not necessarily protect the account owner (the Center) from charges of contempt for failing to produce the tape.[12] The purpose, obviously, is to prevent police and prosecutory authorities access to the named files. There is nothing currently illegal about this process. And if the scientific purpose of confidentiality is paramount, such a process is both pragmatically expedient and ethical. In research such as described here, researchers should be cautioned not to record the names of victims or other identifying facts about specific crimes unless absolutely essential for the research. Without such details, the files are rendered less useful to law-enforcement officials.

We have considered some ethical issues of research in criminology and have used a specific project to illustrate them. More questions have been raised than current philosophy and practice answer. Still, within the confines of the case study, firm responses have been given, and they side with refusal to reveal knowledge about crimes committed by a subject population questioned for research purposes.

NOTES

1. For a summary review about researchers who may be covered in a model shield statute, see Paul Nejelski and Howard Peyser, "A Researcher's Shield Statute: Guarding Against the Compulsory Disclosure of Research Data," Appendix B in *Protecting Individual Privacy in Evaluation Research*, the Committee on Federal Agency Evaluation Research, Assembly of Behavioral and Social Sciences, National Research Council, Washington, D.C.: National Academy of Sciences, 1975.

2. Marvin E. Wolfgang, Robert M. Figlio, Thorsten Sellin, *Delinquency in a Birth Cohort*, Chicago: University of Chicago Press, 1972. See also Marvin E. Wolfgang, "Crime in a Birth Cohort," *Proceedings of the American Philosophical Society* (1973) 117:5:404-11.

3. F.H. McClintock, "The Dark Figure," *Collected Studies in Criminological Research*, Council of Europe, 1970, pp.13-27, 31-34.

4. James F. Short Jr. and F. Ivan Nye, "Reporting Behavior as a Criterion of Deviant Behavior," *Social Problems* (1957-58) 5:207-13.

5. Robert H. Hardt and George E. Bodine, *Development of Self-Report Instruments in Delinquency Research: A Conference Report*, Syracuse, New York: Syracuse University Press, 1965.

6. Martin Gold, *Status Forces in Delinquent Boys*, Ann Arbor, Michigan: Institute for Social Research, University of Michigan, 1963; also Martin Gold, "Undetected Delinquent Behavior," *Journal of Research in Crime and Delinquency* (1966) 3:27-46.

7. Austin L. Porterfield, "Delinquency and Its Outcome in Court and College," *American Journal of Sociology* (1943) 49:199-208; also Austin L. Porterfield, *Youth in Trouble*, Austin, Texas: Leo Potishman Foundation, 1946.

8. Publication of the Kinsey Institute's material (Institute for Sex Research) in the late 1940s and early 1950s produced a considerable amount of concern with maintaining the confidence of the subjects interviewed. The Institute's staff, after publication, have indicated that in the absence of judicial recognition of a privilege between a researcher and his subject, the information would be destroyed and the Institute would accept the consequences, see Nejelski and Peyser, B-12.

9. Researchers are not granted judicial protection based on the First Amendment. In *Branzburg v. Hayes*, 408 U.S. 665 (1972) the court rejected a reporter's privilege based on that amendment. However, there are some narrow areas of protection, as in the case of research on the effect and use of drugs, according to the Federal Comprehensive Drug Abuse Prevention Control Act of 1970.

10. See Nejelski and Peyser in the section entitled "Persons Covered," p.B-5-B-6.

11. Alfred Blumstein, *Science and Technology*, Task Force Report of the President's Commission on Law Enforcement and the Administration of Justice, 1967.

12. Similar issues have been raised in Marvin E. Wolfgang, "The Social Scientist in Court," Journal of Criminal Law and Criminology (1974) 65:2:239-47.

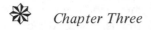 *Chapter Three*

Ethics, The "Hidden Side" of Bureaucracy, and Social Research

Gideon Sjoberg

Bureaucratic structures loom ever more powerful and affect, in subtle and not-so-subtle ways, the destiny of most persons within industrial-urban orders. Although the activities of bureaucracies have been analyzed at considerable length by a variety of scholars, a number of stragetic issues await clarification. Not the least of these are the actions associated with the "hidden side" of bureaucratic organizations.

To explore this problem area, we must first understand how and why a hidden, or secret, side to bureaucracy comes to be a rather normal state of affairs. This analysis lays the groundwork for examining the impact of bureaucratic secrecy upon such specific issues as privacy, confidentiality, and accountability, and upon "human dignity" more generally. After establishing the contours of these interrelationships, we are in a position to focus upon the ethical and political (including legal) issues involved in conducting research on bureaucracy. Although our primary concern is with patterns within the United States, many of our generalizations hold for other industrial-urban orders and for multinational organizations as well.

THE ROLE OF THE SOCIAL SCIENTIST

Some comments upon the major functions of social scientists should clarify the assumptions that inform this chapter. One task is to formulate empirically based theoretical generalizations about specific social orders, as well as social orders in general. Many social scientists view this as their sole activity. Yet they find themselves expending considerable effort in another role: that is, they collect and dissem- inate data about the characteristics of a society (or societies), its organizations, and its members. Although the critics of social-science research contend, and rightly so, that many of these materials are of marginal worth, it is also apparent that industrial-urban orders possess an insatiable appetite for data about their activities and members. Social surveys, or public-opinion polls more specifically, serve as a guide, at least in delineating the limits of acceptable practice, for persons who formulate certain kinds of public policy. To cite a dramatic instance, the current energy crisis highlights the demand for new and different kinds of data on the political economy of the petroleum and related industries. The information furnished by corporations has been judged incomplete and self-serving, and some policy-makers are calling for greater involvement by the federal government in data-gathering in this area. This could lead to greater involvement by social scientists in the collection and analysis of data on energy-related matters.

But there are other roles that social scientists have played or should play. One is to translate their results for the policy makers.[1] It may not be enough simply to gather and analyze data, for these require interpretation if they are to be meaningful and are to be utilized by legislators, bureaucratic officials, and the like. Moreover, social scientists, or at least some of them, must participate in the construction of alternative social structures and ethical orientations. The future is never fully predetermined, and social scientists have a part to play in shaping a just and moral order. Such an orientation calls into question Weber's "value-free" sociology (to which he was in practice never fully committed) and the logical empiricist's view that ethical systems are essentially metaphysical and as such are not a legitimate scientific concern. Indeed, social scientists are being drawn into a concern with moral issues. Those in the West, for instance, live in societies that are undergoing "moral crises," including a crisis of authority, and a failure to assist in building an alternative moral order could undermine their legitimacy with the public at large. In addition, more adequate ethical theories are required if the ethical codes of social-science associations are to be meaningful, and if the interrelationships of ethics, social theory, and social research are to be understood.

BUREAUCRACY AND ITS HIDDEN SIDE

The hidden side of bureaucracy generates secrecy systems. Yet the practice of secrecy is hardly unique to bureaucracy. In one form or another it has played a salient role in most social systems. We could point to institutionalized patterns of secrecy in many preliterate societies, to a wide variety of secret orders in preindustrial civilized societies, and, above all, to the proliferation of secrecy systems in industrial-urban orders.

Among sociologists, Simmel looms as a central figure in the analysis of secrecy. He advanced our knowledge about the role of secrecy in the structuring of social relationships; however, he contributed relatively little, except indirectly, to our understanding of secrecy systems within the context of large-scale bureaucracies.

The typical bureaucratic structure, if we follow Weber's definition, is characterized by a hierarchy of authority, a division of labor (i.e. a high degree of specialization of functions), rationality (the basis of efficiency), and the fact that authority resides in the office rather than in the person. Although Weber recognized the role of secrecy in bureaucratic settings, his brief discussion riveted attention upon its functioning among rather than within bureaucracies. Nor have Weber's many admirers investigated in any detail the variegated facets of the hidden side of bureaucratic life. As a result social scientists were caught off guard by the Watergate affair and its spillover effects. Although social scientists could not have anticipated the specific contents of this debacle, they should have recognized the existence of the conditions necessary for such a scandal to arise.

The structure of bureaucracy, most notably its hierarchical nature, fosters secrecy in rather specific ways.[2] In order for persons in the upper echelons to sustain power, they must exercise control over the sources and flow of information. Information creates and sustains power. In a bureaucratic hierarchy information is expected to flow upward far more readily than downward. Ideally, the leaders of bureaucracy require a wide array of data if they are to act rationally. But those who command the seats of power often proceed a step further in their reasoning. They conceive of much of their information as "privileged." Consequently, in their judgment, they alone are qualified to take a global perspective and make strategic decisions. They alone are in a position to manage the flow of data, thereby protecting the system from unfair attack from without. They alone are in a position to determine what is best for their particular organization and the broader society.

Admittedly, persons who occupy positions of power (the managers) are expected to delegate responsibility for their decisions to members of the lower echelons. But in practice managers tend to delegate blamability under the guise of responsibility. Ultimately the leaders of bureaucracies expect to receive credit for their actions when these prove to be successful, but when they are unsuccessful they blame subordinates. Such is justified, for instance, on the grounds that the actions of the leaders symbolize the organization to the broader society.

As a result of the pattern of blamability, countervailing structures develop. Subordinates, in order to protect themselves, attempt to control the kinds of information that are disseminated to superiors. This manipulation of information from below leads to an "underside" to bureaucracy, to a pattern of secrecy somewhat different from that in the upper echelons.

The complex division of labor within (and among) bureaucracies only accentuates these secrecy arrangements. The specialization of tasks, so typical of bureaucratic organizations, leads functionaries to amass highly technical (and at times secret) kinds of knowledge. Consequently these specialists demand special privileges. In turn, by restricting the flow of information, specialists can make themselves indispensable to an organization. They are able to limit the power of the leadership to act (even against them) and at the same time ward off the encroachment of competing subgroups.

Not only does the structure of bureaucracy foster secrecy systems, but certain kinds of values, or ideologies, are essential in order to justify these arrangements. Corporate managers, for example, frequently insist upon secrecy as a means of sustaining competition, a central feature of the economic system in capitalist nations. Moreover, the "official statistics" they provide the public are often constructed with an eye to revealing only limited knowledge about the internal operations of the organization. This arrangement is justified as a means of protecting the corporation from its competitors or such potentially hostile organizations as governmental regulatory agencies.

Within the political realm we find similar rationales for the use of secrecy. The overriding justification for secrecy in the federal sphere in the United States, and other nations as well, is protection of "the national interest" or, more narrowly, "national security." Through classification of documents, for instance, attempts are made to restrict information to a narrow range of policy-makers. The classification of information as "secret" can be carried to inordinate lengths. But this should occasion no surprise. When in doubt, bureaucrats, in order to avoid possible blame, will say "No" to any request. So too, rather than risk future culpability, they will classify an item as "secret." This is usually the safest course of action.

An examination of the workings of particular branches of the federal government suggests variations on the above theme. The justification of secrecy as part of "executive privilege" on various occasions protected the executive branch from encroachment by the legislative and judicial arms of the government. Concomitantly, the claim to special privilege also has been supported by the doctrine of national interest.

Appeals to the national interest, or "nationalism," have been adduced by numerous policy-makers in modern societies when called upon to justify their ethical perspectives. A similar argument has been employed by social scientists and members of the legal profession. With the rise of the modern nation-state, in the wake of the Industrial and the French revolutions, nationalism became the overriding ideology in the West. Rephrased as "the national interest," it became the primary basis for rationalizing the presence of secrecy systems within the public sector, not just in the United States but in other nation-states as well. Thus, numerous secret arrangements have come to be protected by the legal structure.

We have observed how bureaucratic structures and the broader value system give rise to a hidden, or secret, side. We should also recognize that once in existence, secrecy systems come to have a life of their own. Many individuals come to have a vested interest in maintaining secret arrangements. In addition, certain secrecy systems in, say, the economic sphere lead to double or triple structures of insulation where one secret organization is protected by another, to the extent that the arrangements may become confusing even to the persons involved.

THE IMPACT OF SECRECY

Secrecy systems, unless subjected to on-going scrutiny, expand and erode democratic values and the very foundations of an open society. Hidden structures within and among bureaucracies are associated with a variety of arrangements that are legal, quasi-legal, or illegal in nature. These function in conjunction with, and often in a manner complementary to, the official bureaucratic organizations.

Secrecy systems are a threat to an open society, for they are highly effective in controlling and manipulating the citizenry without the latter's knowledge. In its most brutal form, in totalitarian states, the secrecy apparatus functions as the primary means for social control.[3] The secret police, secret arrests, secret trials, and secret prisons constitute a formidable machinery for sustaining terror. When a person confronts grave uncertainties in everyday life, a major accommodation is to adhere as closely as possible to official policy. Under these conditions, the secrecy apparatus destroys privacy and confidentiality—indeed, human rights in general, especially for persons who do not occupy positions of power.

But secrecy is not unique to totalitarian orders. As a result of Watergate and its fallout we can more readily grasp, at least in hindsight, the dangers of secrecy in an open society.[4] Watergate has dramatized how a hidden side to the political bureaucracy can emerge and function in modern society, how it can subvert on-going political activities, how it can undermine privacy and confidentiality and breed widespread fear and suspicion within bureaucracies and among the general populace. The difficulties of penetrating the veil of secrecy within and among bureaucracies are documented by Bernstein and Woodward, who, through their investigative reporting, opened up the Watergate.[5]

The rush of events that have followed the Watergate affair have been as informative as the activities that preceded President Nixon's resignation from office. Investigations by the congressional, executive, and judicial branches of the government have documented the fact that federal and state bureaucracies as well as the corporate sector have engaged in a variety of activities that have been hidden from the general public, social scientists, and members of the legal community.

We shall mentioned only some of the implications of the hidden side of public bureaucracies for American society. Surely the institutions that support an open society can be directly threatened. The direct intervention of law-enforcement agencies in the lives of American citizens, particularly political dissenters, has been underscored by a formidable amount of data. The effort to discredit Martin Luther King's actions in behalf of the black community is merely one of the many striking intrusions by law-enforcement officials into the legitimate political sphere during the 1960s.

With the existence of secrecy systems in the governmental sphere, privacy can be undermined, either by the collection of data about persons without their knowledge or through some form of coercion. Through secret arrangements confidentiality can be destroyed e.g. by securing data to which one does not, because of prior agreements with a subject, have legitimate access. Secrecy systems also permit the powerful to avoid being held accountable for their actions. There is the danger that the power groups will claim the privilege of "confidentiality" in order to protect their position or that of the system they command. By evading accountability for their actions that affect the public the powerful subvert the rights of the powerless.

Besides directly influencing the political process, the hidden side to public bureaucracies generates data that cannot be effectively checked by independent observers. Sam Adams in "Vietnam Cover-up: Playing War with Numbers"[6] discusses how the highly dubious estimates of the troop strength of the Vietcong came to be relied upon by various branches of the U.S. government. These statistics, which had little or no basis in empirical reality, came to be treated as "truth" by the society's leaders. Adams describes his inability to convince his superiors in the CIA and high officials in other branches of the intelligence community that the estimates of enemy troop strength were grossly out of line with existing evidence. It can be said, then, that secret organizations develop secrecy systems of their own.

The hidden side of bureaucracy, in its various forms, makes it extremely difficult for journalists or social scientists to gain access to crucial information regarding the workings of many public bureaucracies.[7] On the one hand, the "official releases" are designed to reflect the particular image that an agency's officialdom wishes to project. On the other hand, newsmen, and other interested citizens, find their sources compromised through secrecy structures. Thus, data about phone calls made by a *New York Times* reporter who was suspected of leaking "privileged information" were obtained via a secret subpoena of the American Telephone and Telegraph Company by the Internal Revenue Service.[8] Here we have a situation where a bureaucratic structure, whose store of information had been invaded, attempts through secret avenues to uncover the culprit who had relied upon confidential (i.e. secret) sources for his material. Just how privacy, confidentiality, and accountability are to be achieved under these circumstances is a serious question.

The hidden sides of public bureaucracies find their counterparts in the corporate sector. One has only to read the *Wall Street Journal*, the *New York Times*, and the *Washington Post* to recognize that scandals in the economic sphere are not rare. What I term "the other economy" has come to play a major role in the United States and abroad.[9]

The other economy appears to be especially prevalent in those realms where the public and private bureaucracies intersect. Or, more specifically, where the political and economic systems intersect. Thus, the data that have accumulated on multinational corporations indicate that high-ranking executives have, directly or indirectly, condoned payoffs to political officials in the United States and other nations in order to maximize profits.[10] The government itself may be a customer of bribes, for these ensure that the government officials will draw up the proper contracts or will permit the corporations to bypass any constraints imposed by the political or legal apparatus. One aspect of the last-mentioned pattern occurs when officials are paid off so that poor-quality services can be rendered or inferior-quality products distributed to customers. Thus the grain scandals in the United States reveal a system of payoffs that made it possible to ship inferior-quality grain to other nations, often those which were poor and lacked the facilities for inspecting the imported grain.

Within the United States, it appears that in certain sectors of the economy payoffs are a way of life. They occur in such diverse economic realms as privately owned nursing homes and the construction industry. In New York City contractors appear to take the cost of payoffs into account when they submit their bids.[11] The ill-fated career of ex-vice president Agnew focused attention upon similar patterns within Baltimore County and the state of Maryland. Here we found engineers and architects, who identify with distinguished professional associations, deeply involved in activities that reflect not just a secret but a dark side of the economy.

Economists and other social scientists cannot indefinitely ignore the impact of "the other economy" upon the functioning of the official one. Efforts must be made to analyze the role of this more hidden economy in determining the Gross National Product, employment (and unemployment) figures, and even the nature of international trade.

ETHICS, POLITICS, AND SOCIAL RESEARCH

If social scientists, legal scholars, and government officials are indeed committed to an open society, and if they believe that the economic structure of this kind of social order can in part at least be managed so as to serve the interests of the broader society and humankind, then we must come to terms with the hidden side of the political economy. Surely if the theory and data of social scientists are to be properly evaluated, we can no longer ignore bureaucracy's hidden side.

One question immediately comes to the fore: How can social scientists, in particular, gain access to data on activities which by their very nature are to be kept from public scrutiny? If we examine some of the procedures of investigative journalists—e.g. I.F. Stone, Seymour Hersch, Jack Anderson, and Ralph Nader—we acquire some understanding of how adversary journalists gain access to the hidden side of bureaucratic life.[12] Some of their procedures can be employed by social scientists, and in turn the latter can go beyond the typical journalists by analyzing the issues within a theoretical framework.

Such traditional tools as probability sampling are inapplicable for obtaining information about secrecy systems within and among bureaucracies. Social scientists as well as conventional journalists have generally accepted as true the definitions of reality provided by bureaucratic officialdom. Although investigative journalists can often bypass official definitions, they also bypass procedures that social scientists typically hold dear.

A healthy scepticism must be combined with the recognition that the perspective of the power group often differs from that of persons who hold subordinate positions. Playing off divergent kinds of data—those obtained from official communiqués or through leaks by officials or their subordinates—provides researchers with clues about secrecy systems. Scandals or other major ruptures within the government or in corporations usually provide additional kinds of information, and these data come to exist in newspaper accounts, court records, and congressional hearings. All of these can cast considerable light upon the functioning of the hidden side of bureaucracies.

Certain other principles should also be taken into account. Information must be diffused within and among bureaucracies, if modern industrial-urban orders are to function effectively. And we should realize that bureaucracies are not necessarily monolithic in nature. Materials are accidentally exposed to public scrutiny, because an organization's left hand may not know what the right hand is doing. In addition, rivalries among bureaucracies bring about leaks of information, as one organization (or group) seeks special advantages over another. The journalist I.F. Stone, despite occasional failures, has been a master at decoding the workings of the hidden side of bureaucracies through his scrutiny of a variety of public documents and his search for contradictions in official pronouncements which can indicate the presence of secret activities.

But formulating some general tools for gaining knowledge about the hidden side of bureaucracies constitutes only the initial step. We should also recognize that some of the traditional rules of evidence in social science must be modified. One step is for researchers to recognize that the evidence acquired by reporters, courts, and congressional committees is based upon differing standards. Another step is for social scientists to develop a more effective political base as well as more meaningful ethical systems. It is rather self-evident that universities have not been an effective base for studying the hidden side of political and economic life. So, too, current ethical codes—for instance, that of the American Sociological Association— do little or nothing to provide the researcher with a rationale for securing information about powerful organizations. Indeed, these codes may inhibit such efforts.

Social scientists and lawyers are very often employed to provide special knowledge and skills for persons in power positions; indeed, lawyers frequently become part of the power group itself. Nevertheless, both lawyers and social scientists tend to define their respective tasks in rather narrow terms. By taking loyalty to the system for granted, they often carry out their duties without examining the broader ethical and moral implications of their actions.

I am currently completing a book with Ted R. Vaughan—"The Sociology of Ethics." Given our perspective, social scientists, and lawyers as well, if they are to sustain themselves in the modern world, must escape from the narrow confines of "system loyalty" as the ultimate basis for defining what is right and what is wrong. Certainly there is built into science a commitment to transnational "truth systems." We proceed further by contending that a set of "transcendental ethical categories" is essential if social scientists are to attain knowledge (or "truth") about modern social orders.

> The transnational ethical categories to which we refer are based not merely upon existing conditions but upon the human potential for creating alternative social arrangements. In part our theory rests upon [George Herbert] Mead's notion of the social nature of the mind and its consequent capacity for reflexivity. As such it diverges, on the one hand, from the writings of Kant and G.E. Moore, who locate ethical concerns in the categorical imperative and in intuition, respectively, and, on the other hand, from the writings of utilitarians such as Bentham and Mill.[13]

Indeed, the ethical theory of utilitarianism in its various forms continues to permeate contemporary literature in sociology and law, although the work of Rawls,[14] for example, seems destined to force a re-evaluation of existing ethical theorizing.

Underlying our orientation is the principle that it is easier for humankind to determine what is wrong than to determine what is right. Ultimately what is "good" or "right" is open-ended. Thus, we contend that human beings are neither "perfect" nor "imperfect"; they are "unperfect," yet amenable to considerable improvement, though they are by no means perfectible.

In light of our ethical stance, we postulate the existence of some absolute wrongs. The practice of genocide, as illustrated by the Nazi destruction of the European Jews, marks the outer limit of what is morally wrong. Even scientists who contend that their actions should be "value free" seem willing to concede that genocide is morally wrong. To do otherwise would be to condone the possible ultimate destruction of their own social order and consequently of their own scientific endeavors.

Although awareness of the outer limits of immoral action may be of limited worth in a number of practical situations, it nonetheless calls attention to the transnational nature of the human condition and provides us with some standard(s) for evaluating actions in terms other than those which are specific to a particular sociocultural setting. A transcendental ethical orientation provides a check upon persons who define research activities within the narrow confines of a particular nation-state, without reference to broader principles of human dignity.

> We predicate our theory upon the principle of human dignity—a principle that has both a "value" and a "structural" component. The ultimate attack upon human dignity is deprivation of human status, which found its extreme form in the genocidal policies of Nazi Germany. In the area of structure, human dignity is denied when persons are not permitted to make significant choices or to exert significant control over the organizations that have an impact upon their lives.[15]

Although totalitarian states provide us with the extreme cases resulting from the definition of persons as nonhuman, other societies are not without ethical flaws. Consider the syphilis experiment in Alabama described in the following quotation:

> Since 1932, under the leadership, direction and guidance of the United States Public Health Service, there has been a continuing study, centered in Macon County, Alabama, of the effect of untreated syphilitic infection in approximately 400 Black male human beings infected with syphilis as subjects. In the pursuit of this study approximately 200 Black male human beings without syphilis were followed as controls.[16]

This experiment continued for about forty years, long after an effective treatment for this disease had been discovered. The black subjects were, I suspect, viewed initially, at least by some persons in control of the experiment, as nonhumans, and the lack of public discussion served to keep the program in operation over the years. More generally, serious ethical issues arise in situations where bureaucracy defines its clients as nonhuman and thus expendable.

As for the structural dimension to human dignity, people must be in a position to maximize choices (though not at the expense of other persons) and to construct alternatives. Such an orientation implies more than psychological freedom. Sociologic and legal scholars often define freedom as adherence to norms: humans are free when they accept "what is." But only where *structural alternatives* are maximized (given existing sociocultural conditions) can we rightly speak of human dignity being attainable.

The effort by Vaughan and myself to formulate a sociology of ethics, with emphasis upon human dignity, is congruent with the struggle of many contemporary intellectuals to escape from the prison of cultural relativism. Although the ethic of cultural relativism did force intellectuals and policy-makers to consider members of other sociocultural orders in a more positive light, this orientation created its own dilemmas, not the least of which is expressed in the slogan "My nation (or organization), right or wrong." The Nuremberg trials, the Eichmann trial in Jerusalem,[17] the U.N. Declaration of Human Rights, and the efforts of some intellectuals to defend transnational values all mirror a movement away from cultural relativism, at a time when people throughout the world are coming to share a common fate.

Social scientists and legal scholars are required to play a positive role in the construction and application of an ethical orientation that is committed to human rights and human dignity—not merely system maintenance—if they are to justify effectively the study of the hidden side of modern bureaucracies and face up to the issues generated by the impact of secrecy systems upon the need for privacy and confidentiality for individuals, as well as hold officials accountable for their "public activities."

Inasmuch as persons in positions of power in a bureaucracy can through the use of secrecy manipulate those below—in effect treating them as objects to rationalize the organization's immediate goals—the question of the ethical propriety of such an arrangement must be brought to the fore. If more humane social orders are to develop, social scientists must not uncritically accept the view that a bureaucratic power group can define its freedom at the expense of subordinates, including clients.

We should constantly keep in mind the relationships among confidentiality, privacy, accountability, bureaucracy, and the ethics of social research. Researchers have in recent years become sensitive to the need for preserving the confidentiality of their research sources and findings. But they have typically failed to recognize that through its hidden side a bureaucracy can gain access to this information and use it to its own advantage. A number of files, we can safely assume, have been created under the assumption that the data therein concerning individuals would remain confidential. However, power groups within bureaucracies can through secret agreements undermine the confidentiality of information. At the same time they themselves may maintain their own secret files, which they protect and which inform their actions. How accountability of public officials under these circumstances can be achieved has yet to be determined. These facts continue to be skirted by social scientists and legal scholars, because of their inadequate understanding of the workings of the hidden side of bureaucracy.

More specifically, the problems posed by databanks are informa- tive. The study *Databanks in a Free Society*[18] points up some of the complexities involved. However, the authors fail to face up to the issue of how databanks are to be protected against misuse by persons who, as a result of special roles within the hidden side of bureau- cracy, are able to break computer codes,[19] feed in false data, etc. It is all too easy to assume that information labeled as confidential will be treated as such by persons who are part of an organization's hidden, and sometimes illegal, side.

How are social researchers to cope with such subversion of confidentiality and even of accountability? First, we must gain a better understanding of how bureaucracy actually functions. In light of what we have learned in recent years, more consideration should be given to the dangers inherent in the centralization of information about individuals in the hands of bureaucratic officials. Concom- itantly, more attention should be given to using social research and theory as one means of holding public officials accountable, not merely for system maintenance but also for protecting human rights and human dignity. Social research, including more effective theo- rizing about bureaucracy, is one way of exposing the negative consequences of bureaucracy's hidden side to public scrutiny.

Nevertheless, researchers find it difficult to justify holding the leaders of bureaucracies accountable, simply on the basis of informa- tion about how their official activities are related to bureaucracy's hidden side. One rationale can be found in appeals to freedom of speech and the press. Or social scientists can refer to the ideal of the dissemination of knowledge. The ethic of human dignity, however, strikes more directly at the issues involved. It is in keeping with the universal nature of scientific endeavor. It challenges the assumption that the maintenance of a system, or of a person's power position, should take precedence over human rights, and recognizes the fact that the destinies of people in various social orders are becoming increasingly intertwined.

Still, a compelling ethic alone will not suffice. Social scientists require structural supports if they are to be protected from possible destruction by the bureaucracies they study. As suggested above, the university in the United States, for instance, has proved to be less than satisfactory as a social base for furthering research on powerful bureaucracies. Although efforts to make universities more effective research institutions should be encouraged, we should also build or strengthen other organizational structures, including professional associations.

Most social-science associations have typically assumed a defensive posture with respect to encroachments by the state (or by corporate structures) upon research activities. Recently we have witnessed some interest in making use of these associations in a more positive manner, as vehicles for sustaining research of a controversial nature. But, if we can judge by the experience of the American Sociological Association, the contrast between what is to be done and what has been done is staggering.

The vision of a strong, viable social-science association remains to be constructed. Should social-science associations, for instance, support "shield laws" for researchers? This issue has received little attention from the social-science community. Until greater understanding is reached about the kinds of protection that should be sought, we are well advised to proceed cautiously lest we enact legislation that bureaucracies could employ to their own advantage in protecting their hidden side. During the interim, social scientists and other interested parties should exert maximum effort to ward off legislation that would further inhibit research on powerful bureaucracies. Any attempt by Congress to pass a "state secrets" act should be resisted. At present it is easier to block unfriendly legislation than to enact legislation that will protect investigators in the pursuance of their activities.

The development of national and international associations that serve the cause of human dignity, and not merely the preservation of a power group, is a needed long-run endeavor. To be effective, such associations must be more than mere extensions of powerful bureaucracies. Indeed, an on-going tension between the two kinds of organization is essential, for where integration or consensus reigns, few challenges to the activities of the hidden side of bureaucracies will be made.

SUMMARY

There is a hidden side to all large-scale bureaucracies, and the activities it engenders pose serious impediments, as well as major challenges, to social research and theory building. Social researchers, if they are to remain true to their calling, need to understand the workings of both the public and the hidden sides of powerful bureaucracies. These patterns are significant in their own right as key ingredients in the functioning of modern social orders, but also as threats to an "open society"—especially in the political and economic spheres.

In this theoretical sketch, I have reasoned that such issues as privacy, confidentiality, and accountability cannot be understood apart from the hidden side of powerful bureaucracies; yet these interrelationships have been treated inadequately by social scientists. Moreover, how one proposes to examine privacy, confidentiality, and accountability rests to a large extent upon one's ethical orientation. In this chapter I have suggested an ethical perspective that will serve the cause of human dignity and at the same time provide some guidelines for more informed research upon bureaucratic phenomena.

NOTES

1. See W. Boyd Littrell and Gideon Sjoberg (eds.), *Current Issues in Social Policy Research*, Beverly Hills, Calif.: Sage Publications, forthcoming.

2. For a useful survey of the literature on secrecy and bureaucracy (and for a perspective somewhat different from my own), see Daniel Carl Rigney, "Organizational Secrecy: An Investigation of Hidden Realities," unpublished Ph.D. dissertation, The University of Texas at Austin, 1975.

3. See, e.g., Raul Hilberg, *The Destruction of the European Jews* (Chicago: Quadrangle, 1961). Cf. Aleksandr I. Solzhenitsyn, *The Gulag Archipelago 1918-1956*, New York: Harper & Row, 1974.

4. As a result of Watergate we have a new perspective on the hidden side of political bureaucracies in the United States. The literature on this scandal is enormous, and it continues to grow. For a good one-volume survey see J. Anthony Lukas, *Night-mare*, New York: Viking Press, 1976.

5. Carl Bernstein and Bob Woodward, *All the President's Men*, New York: Simon and Schuster, 1974.

6. Sam Adams, "Vietnam Cover-up: Playing War with Numbers," *Harper's*, 250 (May 1975), 41-73.

7. Some of these issues were brought to the fore in the "Daniel Ellsberg Case." See, e.g., Rigney. Also, for background data on the emerging case of Daniel Schorr, see Daniel Schorr, "My 17 Months on the CIA Watch," *Rolling Stone*, No. 210 (April 8, 1976), 32 ff.

8. E.G. Warren Weaver, Jr., "I.R.S. Will Return Phone-Calls Data," *New York Times*, February 13, 1974, 25. Cf. Paul Cowan *et al.*, *State Secrets*, New York: Holt, Rinehart and Winston, 1974.

9. For a more detailed discussion of "the other economy" see my chapter in Littrell and Sjoberg.

10. In addition to the detailed reports set forth in the newspapers mentioned in the text, the following book provides data as to how the other economy operates on the international scene: Thurston Clarke and John J. Tigue, Jr., *Dirty Money*, New York: Simon and Schuster, 1975.

11. David K. Shipler, "Study Finds $25-Million Yearly in Bribes is Paid by City's Construction Industry," *New York Times*, June 26, 1972, 1+, and David K. Shipler, "City Construction Grafters Face Few Legal Penalties," *New York Times*, June 27, 1972, 1+.

12. Gideon Sjoberg and Paula Jean Miller, "Social Research on Bureaucracy: Limitations and Opportunities," *Social Problems*, 21 (Summer 1973), 129-73.

13. Ted R. Vaughan and Gideon Sjoberg, "Ethics and Social Problems Theory," *The Society for the Study of Social Problems: Social Problems Theory Division Newsletter*, No. 5 (Winter 1976), 32.

14. John Rawls, *A Theory of Justice*, Cambridge, Mass.: Belknap Press, 1971.

15. Vaughan and Sjoberg.

16. *Final Report of the Tuskegee Syphilis Study Ad Hoc Advisory Panel*, Washington, D.C.: U.S. Department of Health, Education, and Welfare, 1973, 18.

17. For a somewhat different perspective on the construction of transnational norms, see Ted R. Vaughan and Gideon Sjoberg, "The Social Construction of Legal Doctrine: The Case of Adolf Eichmann," in Jack D. Douglas, *Deviance and Respectability*, New York: Basic Books, 1970.

18. *Databanks in a Free Society*, Report of the Project on Computer Databanks of the Computer Science and Engineering Board, National Academy of Sciences, New York: Quadrangle/New York Times Book Co., 1973.

19. Donn B. Parker et al., *Computer Abuse*, Prepared for the National Science Foundation, Menlo Park, Calif.: Stanford Research Institute, 1973. Cf, Raymond L. Dirks and Leonard Gross, *The Great Wall Street Scandal*, New York: McGraw-Hill Book Co., 1974. esp. 240 ff. In discussing the fraud perpetrated by Equity Funding Corporation of America, the authors write (p. 241):

A computer produces printouts; each printout, however, may be a refinement of several printouts. The details, in effect, remain inside the computer. Only the final result appears on the printout—not the many calculations and changes that produced it. All that an auditor sees is the final product. He no longer sees the process by which it was achieved.

There were no phony files for the funded program. The only instruments of deception were the computer and its output.

✳ *Chapter Four*

Invading the Government's Privacy: Problems of Research on National Security Issues

Carol Barker

Since the Sunday in May 1971 when the *New York Times* published the first segment of the Pentagon history of U.S. decision-making in Vietnam, the federal government's system of protecting sensitive national defense and foreign policy information through security classification and the political uses and abuses of that system have become major political issues. Information has become ammunition in the battle over the substance and control of U.S. foreign policy that developed out of the bitter disputes over the war in Indochina. Overshadowed by the larger controversies but involved and affected by them were independent scholars—those without government affiliation—doing research on postwar and contemporary U.S. foreign and defense policy.

Even before the publication of the Pentagon Papers, some of these historians and political scientists had begun to voice publicly their frustrations with the barriers erected by government bureaucracy to research on the government and its policies. They argued that protection of national security information, some of it more than a quarter of a century old, was excessive. They complained about the inconvenient and embarrassing security requirements imposed for scholarly use of classified archives. Some scholars denounced the practice that permitted former officials to write memoirs based on classified information unavailable to private researchers, and thus to shape the public's interpretation of events. Others criticized the government for making classified files available to selected scholars and not to others. They censured as well the scholars who benefited from this discrimination and published research based in large part on nonpublic and therefore unverifiable evidence. The issues at dispute included the public's right to information about the functioning of the government; the government's obligation to inform the public and at the same time to protect from dissemination information potentially detrimental to the national interest; and the scholar's responsibility to seek and disseminate information and his responsibility to disclose the sources of his information and the methods by which he obtained it in order to permit other scholars to test his conclusions.

Events since the publication of the Pentagon Papers have had both favorable and adverse effects on the ability of scholars to do research on national security topics. Executive branch reform of the classification system has promised some reduction in the amount of information classified and an accelerated pace of declassification. Congressional passage over a presidential veto of amendments to the Freedom of Information Act in 1974 has already resulted in greater official responsiveness to public requests for classified records. But leaks about the secret bombing of Cambodia in 1969 followed by the Pentagon Papers affair and more recent revelations of the domestic and foreign activities of the intelligence agencies have also increased the anxiety of security-conscious executive branch officials—and in the case of leaks of the House Intelligence Committee's report to the *New York Times* and CBS-TV reporter Daniel Schorr, Congress as well. In the course of the government's investigation of the publication of the Pentagon history of Vietnam decision-making, several scholars received subpoenas to appear before grand juries, and one political scientist spent eight days in jail rather than reveal to a grand jury the names of confidential government sources. The Nixon and Ford administrations endorsed legislation that would make the unauthorized disclosure of classified information—to anyone for any purpose—a crime. Although the passage of this United States version of an official-secrets act at this time seems unlikely, the serious consideration given to it for two years indicates the vulnerability of research on national security topics, which benefits from informal contacts and unauthorized exchange of information between officials and scholars.

Research on national-security topics by its very nature brings the scholar into a close and potentially uncomfortable relationship with the government. Problems of access and control of information may arise any time the government is necessary to facilitate research and is itself the object of research. These difficulties are aggravated in the case of national security, where the executive branch of the government enjoys a near monopoly of information, protected by the classification system and other security devices, and has at its disposal powerful justifications for maintaining its secrecy.

Few challenge the responsibility of the government to prevent serious injury to the defense or diplomatic interests of the nation by protecting sensitive technical or operational information of use to potential or actual enemies, and by maintaining the privacy of current diplomatic communications and ongoing negotiations and the confidentiality of advice or opinion offered in the formulation of policy. (This last justification applies throughout the government but has special force for the foreign-policy establishment, wounded by the attacks of the McCarthy era and more recently shaken by efforts to assign responsibility for the errors of U.S. policy in Southeast Asia.) Congress recognized these responsibilities by exempting information related to national defense and foreign policy classified by executive order from the mandatory provisions of the Freedom of Information Act, which established the public's right to government information.

But events of recent years have demonstrated that the executive branch cannot be allowed to monopolize information about national security if Congress is to exercise its constitutional powers in foreign affairs and if the public is to hold the government ultimately responsible for its policies. The scholar, like the journalist, has a role to play in disseminating information not otherwise available and in providing an independent assessment of government policy. Scholars advocating greater access to national-security information or protection of their confidential sources have identified their particular interests in research free from government control with a public interest in information about the processes and decisions that underly government policy. Testifying before a Congressional committee, historian Lloyd C. Gardner argued for earlier access to classified files in the following terms:

> Nations, like individuals, depend in part upon memory in order to be able to function rationally in the present. Historians are to a degree responsible for what stands out in a nation's memory; they supply experience longer than one generation's lifespan, and broader than that of any group of individuals.
>
> As one approaches the present, the historian's most valuable asset, perspective, is diminished chronologically, and in a secrecy-conscious nation, by the lack of available evidence as well.
>
> The nation's memory is thus weakest for the years of the recent past, a serious defect, unless one is prepared to concede that the public should reach its conclusions on the basis of little or no information, or that the policy-maker is the only one who needs the memory.[1]

Political scientist Hans J. Morgenthau gave even greater emphasis to the researcher's public obligations in testifying in favor of the privilege of confidentiality for scholars dealing with contemporary issues:

> The position of the scholar dealing with contemporary issues is analogous to that of the journalist in that both must rely upon confidential sources for the gathering of facts. . . . The political scientist who would want to probe into the validity and background of a particular policy would be in the same position. For instance, the scholar who has concluded on the basis of his understanding of history and of his general knowledge of political and military theory that a particular war cannot be won with the means employed will find his arguments greatly enriched and his confidence in the soundness of his judgment considerably strengthened if he has access to government sources supplying him with empirical data that support his judgment. To refer to my personal experience, I would not have dared to pit my own judgment about the Vietnam war against that of the Government and the prevailing public and scholarly opinion had I not received confidential information, sometimes from highly placed sources, that bore out my judgment. . . . The functions the journalist or the independent scholar perform are not only useful and necessary but vital for American democracy. For they have become the main channels of independent information and judgment from the opposition within the Government to the people at large.[2]

The tensions inherent in the relationship between government and scholar are naturally intensified when the government's policies are subject to widespread criticism, as they were during the decade of United States involvement in Southeast Asia. Officials may interpret (and may be correct in doing so) the historian's interest in a second look at the decisions and policies that shaped the Cold War posture of the United States at home and abroad as evidence of skepticism about the fundamental assumptions underlying U.S. foreign policy. Similarly, they may suspect that the political scientist's interest in investigating foreign-policy decisions in order to identify patterns of organizational and political behavior may start from the premise or result in the conclusion that the decision-making process is not functioning well and should be changed in order to produce different policies. Those in authority are likely to cherish their monopoly of information and use it to promote a favorable assessment of their activities. Independent and critical research is one counter to this tendency. The abundant evidence of the use of official secrecy by successive administrations in the postwar period to deceive and manipulate public opinion provides sufficient argument for erring, if necessary, on the side of public access and disclosure.

PROBLEMS OF ACCESS

The scholar's commitment to open access and disclosure brings with it special risks and responsibilities when the information is politically sensitive. The first problem is obtaining authorized access to national-security information, which is controlled and strictly limited by the government. There is little dispute that the system of security classification, established in 1951 and with some modifications in existence until 1972, protected too much information for too long. The use of the security stamp became office routine in much of Washington, a means of enhancing the prestige of those who used it, of signaling the importance of an official communication, of protecting questionable policies and covert operations from public and congressional scrutiny, of covering up official blunders. With virtually all national-security information "born classified," selective disclosure became an important tactic in shaping policy.

By one estimate, the page-by-page review of the vast deposit of records classified in the last three decades would require at least another thirty years.[3] Until 1972, there was no systematic, government-wide procedure for declassification review, which after all was not worth the time and expense to officials who already had access to the classified information they needed. The closest approximation to such a review was that carried out by the historical office of the State Department in preparation for the compilation of the annual volumes of the *Foreign Relations of the United States* (FRUS), the department's publication of the significant foreign-policy documents of the United States. In 1972, the State Department was publishing the FRUS volumes for 1946, twenty-six years in the distant past. The State Department also observed a thirty-year limit on the classification of its records, which were then transferred to the National Archives for public use.

The Freedom of Information Act provided the private citizen with a means of initiating the declassification of records, but classified information was exempt from the law's mandatory-disclosure requirements. Given the legislative exemption, the courts refused to review executive-branch classification decisions under the Freedom of Information Act. The utility of the Freedom of Information Act was further diminished by the requirement that those seeking information request "identifiable" records: not only is it difficult for a private citizen to identify a secret record, but scholars usually seek a large number of documents relating to a specific issue. Access to still classified files was permitted under security restrictions to scholars engaged in historical-research projects on the condition that "access to the information will be clearly consistent with the interests of national defense" and "the person to be granted access is trustworthy."[4] Even with these restrictions, departmental rules limited access for the most part to files more than twenty-five years of age.

While public access to classified information was practically nonexistent for postwar documents, there was no lack of information about U.S. foreign policy and defense released by the government through official pronouncements and publications, press conferences, news releases, interviews, and off-the-record briefings. Of particular importance was the practice of "leaking" classified information to newsmen, and to scholars as well. These confidential disclosures by officials high and low served a variety of bureaucratic purposes: enhancement of reputations, testing of new ideas without accepting premature responsibility for them, solicitation of public support in intragovernmental disputes, or the sabotaging of opposing positions. Former officials continued that practice by using classified information in their memoirs or inside accounts of events in which they participated. These practices served the public by providing not otherwise available information, but not well, since the information released in this way was selected, partial, and out of context. Since disclosure or publication was not the equivalent of declassification, the documentary evidence did not become available for independent assessment and interpretation.

The publication of the Pentagon Papers and the administration's reaction to this and other unauthorized leaks were evidence that the system was no longer even serving official interests. In March 1972, President Nixon issued an executive order initiating the first major reform of the classification system in nearly twenty years.[5]

To combat excessive classification, Executive Order 11652, which went into effect on June 1, 1972, called for a reduction in the number of departments and the number of officials within each department with the authority to classify documents. In May 1975, the Interagency Classification Review Committee (ICRC), established by the new order to supervise its implementation, reported in its third annual review that the number of persons authorized to classify documents had been reduced by nearly 75 percent, from over 59,000 to less than 15,500, a number considered to be close to the bare minimum for reasons of administrative efficiency.[6] The new order, and the National Security Council directive implementing it, emphasized personal responsibility for classification, warned against the use of classification for nonsecurity purposes, and encouraged the use of the least restrictive treatment possible in each case of classification.

Whether these provisions will be rigorously and faithfully enforced, and whether they will actually succeed in reducing the amount of information classified, remains to be seen. Although the ICRC review noted a downward trend in the number of documents classified, it also reported over four million classification actions in 1974.[7] An American Civil Liberties Union project that is monitoring the implementation of Executive Order 11652 and the Freedom of Information amendments reports evidence that executive-branch officials are unaware of the stricter guidelines of the new order.[8]

Executive Order 11652 also provided for earlier and more systematic declassification. Whenever possible, at the time of classification, a specific date for declassification is to be indicated on the document. The order established a general declassification schedule of ten, eight, and six years respectively for "top secret," "secret," and "confidential" documents classified under the new order. The existence of a number of exemptions to the general schedule raises the question of whether the new declassification schedule will prove more effective than the twelve-year schedule it replaced. Given the weight of bureaucratic incentives in favor of secrecy, what are meant to be maximum limits on classification may turn out to be minimums. The provision for automatic declassification of all material after thirty years except for information personally exempted by the head of the originating department is a cautious but nevertheless significant improvement over the former practice of indefinite classification.

All of these provisions, however, are for the future, since they apply only to information classified under the new order. Most information classified before June 1972 under Executive Order 10501 is exempt from the ten-year declassification schedule, but is subject to the thirty-year limit on classification. The Archivist of the United States and the departments are given responsibility for systematic review of "all information and material . . . determined . . . to be of sufficient historical or other value to warrant preservation . . . for the purpose of making such information and material publicly available." Painstaking page-by-page review of this vast accumulation of papers, no matter how old, is required before declassification. The National Archives' review of classified documents dating from World War II has already resulted in declassification of 125 million pages, although the program missed its original completion date of December 1975. The new order also specifically authorizes the archivist for the first time to declassify White House papers housed in presidential libraries and other archives. Other departments are also reviewing their stores of classified documents.

For example, the CIA is in the process of declassifying OSS documents from World War II, and the State Department has instituted a review of "top secret" documents dating from 1955 to 1963.[9]

The innovation of Executive Order 11652 that has the most immediate potential for increasing public access to classified records is the provision for mandatory declassification review for all documents more than ten years of age. Any member of the public or department of the government can initiate such a review providing that "the request describes the record with sufficient particularity to enable the Department to identify it" and "the record can be obtained with only a reasonable amount of effort." The implementing directive describes a three-tiered review and appeal process from the departmental classification review office, to a departmental review committee, and finally after ninety days to the ICRC.

The ICRC reported that in 1974, the departments had received 1017 mandatory-declassification review requests, of which 88 percent were granted in full or in part. Less than one percent of the requests were appealed to the ICRC. These requests sometimes involved single documents and sometimes large sets of documents. For example, in its report to the ICRC, one department stated that it had granted 137 requests in one quarter of 1974, which resulted in the release of 4900 documents amounting to approximately 20,000 pages.[10] This optimistic report contradicts the experience of the *New York Times*, which after months of delay and considerable expense received only five of fifty-one sets of documents requested in 1973, one after appeal and reappeal. The *Times'* requests involved large volumes of documents on a given issue rather than specific individual documents. The acting chairman of the ICRC emphasized that the mandatory-declassification review procedures "were not intended to and cannot solve the problem of large volume classification." Large-scale declassification must await the thirty-year review.[11]

Like the *New York Times*, scholars are likely to want access to files of documents on a particular issue rather than individual documents. They may lack the financial resources (three sets of documents released by the State Department cost the *Times* $194) available to the *Times*. In the past, scholars interested in research on national-security records less than thirty years old could apply for security-restricted access to departmental files. Executive Order 11652 permitted the continuation of this system, but the State Department, which had maintained the most important program of this kind, has now eliminated it. As the annual volumes of *FRUS* are released, the documents for that year are transferred to the National Archives and are available there for purposes of research. Although in 1972, President Nixon ordered a reduction in the lag in *FRUS* publication to twenty years by 1975, the department has only managed to schedule the last volumes for 1949 and the first four for 1950 for publication in the summer of 1976, a lag of twenty-six years. The primary means of access to State Department documents dated from 1950 to the present has become the Freedom of Information Act.[12] (The Attorney General's Memorandum on the 1974 Amendments to the Freedom of Information Act advises the departments to process requests for information under the provisions of the amended law rather than Executive Order 11652, unless specifically requested to do otherwise.)[13]

The 1974 amendments of the Freedom of Information Act[14] passed by Congress over a presidential veto are the most important reform to date in the system of gaining access to national-security information. Provisions designed to facilitate access to all sorts of government records may be of some assistance to those seeking national-security documents. The legislation eases the burden on the individual seeking information by changing the requirement that records requested be "identifiable" to a requirement that they be "reasonably described." Agencies must establish a uniform schedule of reasonable fees limited to the direct costs of searching for and copying documents requested under the act. Shorter time limits on agency responses to requests for records are mandated, and Freedom of Information Act cases are to be given precedence by the courts. The courts are given authority to order the government to pay "reasonable attorney fees and other litigation costs" of citizens who successfully litigate cases under the act. "Arbitrary and capricious" withholding of documents is subject to administrative penalties. The most important change from the point of view of scholars seeking access to classified documents is the clarification of the original intent of the legislation by permitting courts in suits brought under the act to examine agency records in camera to determine whether the records are properly withheld under any of the nine permissive exemptions. The legislation thus affirms the authority of the courts to examine classified records to determine whether they "are in fact properly classified pursuant to" an executive order "in the interest of national defense or foreign policy." In addition to these specific provisions, the passage of the legislation should alone serve as an inducement for officials to give greater weight to the need for access in making declassification decisions under the Freedom of Information Act.

A number of significant documents have been released in the year since the implementation of the amendments including the Negotiating Volumes of the Pentagon Papers, background press conferences of the Secretary of State on SALT and the Middle East, assurances from the U.S. government to respond to ceasefire violations in South Vietnam, the Colby Report to President Ford on CIA domestic activities, and investigative files on Alger Hiss and the Rosenbergs, which have been released because of modifications in the seventh exemption covering investigatory records compiled for law-enforcement purposes. A number of suits have been filed to test the national-security exemption to the act.[15] Although requests can be made for large sets of documents, the search and copying fees can make this a costly procedure. The Freedom of Information Act is therefore best suited for the acquisition of individual documents.[16]

Important as the Freedom of Information Act amendments are for obtaining access to classified information, they are no substitute for a reduction in the amount of classification in the first case. The abuses in the classification system revealed over the years, especially after the disclosure of the Pentagon Papers, led to congressional consideration of reforming the classification system by statute. A number of bills with this purpose were introduced in both houses of Congress in the 93rd Congress, but none were reported out of committee. They were characterized by reduction in the number of authorized classifiers, stricter definitions of the criteria for classification, accelerated schedules for declassification, limits on the duration of classification less than the executive order's thirty-year limit, and review and oversight of the classification system by Congress or an independent regulatory agency. These bills basically took over the executive system of classification that has been in effect with modifications since 1951 and proposed a statutory basis for it. They were criticized for not going far enough in limiting what could be classified, and for neglecting to define categories of information that must be disclosed to Congress and the public.[17] The 94th Congress, preoccupied by the abuses of the intelligence agencies, had not reintroduced any of these bills or substitutes for them.

The Murphy Commission on the Organization of the Government for the Conduct for Foreign Policy, in its June 1975 final report, recommended a legislated classification system, which "while fully responsive to the executive's legitimate requirements for secrecy in foreign policy, should balance those interests more evenly against the nation's rights to examine what is being done in its name, and why."[18] To accomplish these purposes, the commission recommended that Congress create a classification system with mandatory-classification categories primarily for national defense and intelligence information, exemptions from classification for any information related principally to U.S. actions in violation of U.S. law, and specific criteria for balancing the need for secrecy against the value of disclosure for all information not falling in either of the two mandatory categories. The commission also recommended that congressional committees assume oversight for the functioning of the system, and that penalties for unauthorized release of properly classified information and administrative sanctions for overclassification be imposed.[19]

Reforms such as those proposed by the Murphy Commission are commendable because they recognize that basic change will only come if executive discretion to classify is limited. Unfortunately, the language of the Murphy Commission still suggests that classification is the rule and disclosure the exemption, and overclassification a lesser abuse than unauthorized disclosure.

THE PROBLEMS OF USE

In summary, Executive Order 11652 in combination with the prospective changes in the Freedom of Information Act has the effect of facilitating declassification of documents in three categories. Documents less than ten years old can be released through the mechanism of the Freedom of Information Act. Requests for reasonably limited and identifiable sets of records more than ten years old may also be satisfied through the mandatory-declassification review procedures of Executive Order 11652. Records of the early postwar period will slowly but surely see the light of day in the next few years through the FRUS publications and the thirty-year declassification rule. Aside from the expenditure of time and money, the use of records declassified in these ways poses no particular problem for the scholar. Declassified records are available to anyone who bothers to learn of their existence and citable like any other written documents.

But despite these advances, the scholar interested in research on national-security topics will still find that for the near future national-security records will remain officially classified for thirty years. Faced with these barriers, those interested in researching issues of recent defense and foreign-policy and policy formulation can proceed in several ways. They can rely exclusively on information in the public domain, avoiding the problems of access to and use of confidential information. This route is not as inhibiting as one might suppose: as in the case of the Pentagon Papers, the classified record may serve primarily to confirm and embellish information already in the public domain.

For some scholars, primarily historians, security-restricted research in the archives of those departments that still permit such access provides a partial answer. Because this officially sanctioned access is restricted for the most part to documents close to the thirty-year classification limit, it is of little use to most scholars of more recent events. The disadvantages of this approach include delays for purposes of security clearance, limits on note-taking, and requirements for review of notes and manuscript. Classified information obtained in this way cannot be published or cited without authorization. Since access for historical-research purposes does not serve a political objective and is managed by archivists rather than policy-makers, the possibility of manipulation for nonsecurity purposes is small. Such access in principal is open to any qualified and trustworthy scholar. Material available to one scholar should be available to all, although the decentralized management of the access programs may result in some inequities. In the past, historical research done under official auspices in classified files has resulted in declassification of documents used in the research, a practice scholars should encourage.

A third approach is the increasingly popular reliance on interviews with participants in policy formulation, both inside and outside government, usually on a not-for-attribution, confidential basis. Scholars have found officials willing to discuss the policy process and their roles in it on this basis, and have in this way been able to bring systematic research to bear on recent policy problems otherwise left to the journalist. Cooperative officials have not infrequently taken the next step and offered scholars access to classified records on an unofficial and confidential basis. A recent spectacular example of research based on not-for-attribution interviews with government officials is an article on Secretary of State Kissinger's step-by-step diplomacy in the Middle East published in *Foreign Policy*, which contains verbatim accounts of conversations between the Secretary of State and his interlocutors in the Middle East and describes secret commitments made by presidents Nixon and Ford in the course of discussions with Arab heads of state.[20]

A number of books published on the U.S. intervention in the Dominican Republic in 1965 illustrate the problems of bureaucratic and scholarly ethics involved in the unauthorized use of secret information in research.[21] Two accounts of the Dominican crisis written by journalists contained information from classified cables sent from the U.S. Embassy in Santo Domingo to Washington. The authors of three scholarly books on the Dominican events also benefited from access to State Department classified files on a confidential basis. But when a fourth scholar, author of a critical study of the Dominican intervention, petitioned the State Department for access to the same files, his request was refused. The recipients of classified information did not use regular channels for requesting access to or declassification of classified information. The Historical Office of the State Department emphatically denied releasing any such information to anyone; as well it might, since the information was obtained through "leaks" from individuals holding policy positions in the State Department on the condition that the classified information would not be cited nor its source revealed.

The Dominican case, like other instances of scholarly use of leaks of classified information, can be interpreted in two different ways. Such leaks can be seen as deliberate government manipulation of scholarly research for political purposes. The bureaucrats involved clearly violate their own security regulations and standards of equity in releasing classified information to selected scholars and denying it to others. The scholars, in this interpretation, become accomplices in a political game in which they compromise scholarly standards of evidence and fair play. Despite their protestations of good faith, their findings become suspect. This interpretation carries some weight in the Dominican case, in particular, because the Johnson administration decision to intervene in the Dominican crisis was so bitterly disputed. Under the circumstances, administration officials might well have wanted to obtain public hearing for their version of events without having to publicly defend it.

But the use of classified leaks by scholars demands a different interpretation in the context of the excessive secrecy surrounding U.S. foreign policy in recent years. The administration has sufficient means to place its version of events before the public, but the classification system prevents public evaluation of raw, undigested information about government policies and practices. The bureaucrat who leaks such information, whatever his motive, is therefore performing a public service. In this context, the scholar has an obligation to use classified information when it is made available to him despite the less-than-ideal conditions imposed on its use. If necessary, the scholar should agree, in this view, to forego citation of his evidence as long as he is free to interpret it in his own way without official interference. The general critical interpretation of U.S. policy in the Dominican crisis presented by some of the books using classified sources lends support to this interpretation.

While the motives for scholarly use of classified information are probably seldom so singularly public-spirited as this second version suggests, such research does serve a useful purpose in helping to penetrate the blanket of secrecy shrouding recent U.S. foreign policy. But the justification for the use of such irregular sources of information imposes additional responsibility on scholars who accept it.

This type of research conflicts with the traditional standards of documentary research, requiring full and careful citation of sources, to which history, and political science to some extent, are accustomed. The standards of empirical social-science research, which require the protection of the confidentiality of sources and depend instead on the description of methods to establish the reliability of data, are not easily applied to research on specific historical events not usefully presented in anonymous or aggregate form.[22] If permission cannot be obtained for the citation of evidence, the careful scholar tries to find independent—if possible public and citable—confirmation for information obtained on a confidential basis. Without citable evidence, the researcher must prevail on the reader's good faith in the reliability of his reportage and judgment.

In addition to his responsibility to the reader, the scholar also has a professional responsibility to protect the free flow of information. Sources of confidential information within the bureaucracy were apparently the targets of a 1972 investigation of Samuel Popkin, a political scientist then at Harvard University who was doing research on Vietnam, by a federal grand jury in Boston convened to examine the events surrounding the unauthorized publication of the Pentagon Papers. Professor Popkin, claiming a testimonial privilege equivalent to a journalist's, refused to answer questions about his confidential government sources. The appeals court refused to recognize such a privilege and upheld Popkin's conviction for contempt. Since the classification system protects so much information that should be in the public domain, scholars should be prepared to make sacrifices to protect those who release information.

The protection of confidential government sources is a less-than-ideal solution from both the scholar's and the citizen's point of view. Far preferable would be an end to a system that permits the government to hide its operations and policies from the public view. As a first step, scholars might make more use of the existing procedures for declassifying documents, thus increasing the amount of information publicly available. The use of classified information should be a last resort after every effort is made to obtain its release by declassification. Scholars should also support reform of the classification system which effectively and narrowly restricts the kinds of information that can be classified in the first place, as well as one that accelerates the pace of declassification. Without such reforms, scholarly use of classified information is likely to increase, and with it the potential for government interference in and manipulation of scholarly research.

NOTES

1. Cited in House Report 93-221, 93rd Congress, 1st session, "Executive Classification of Information—Security Classification Problems Involving Exemption (b) (1) of the Freedom of Information Act (5 U.S.C. 552)," p. 93.

2. Cited in Hearings, Subcommittee on Constitutional Rights of the Committee on the Judiciary, U.S. Senate, 93rd Congress, 1st session, on S.36, etc., Bills to Create a Testimonial Privilege for Newsman, February 20, 21, 22, 27, March 13 and 14, 1973, pp. 392-93.

3. David R. Young, "Secrecy and Disclosure: Breaking the Classification Machine," *Prologue: Journal of the National Archives* (Spring 1973), p. 41.

4. Executive Order 10816, Code of Federal Regulations, III (1959-63 Compilation), pp. 351-52.

5. Executive Order 11652, Code of Federal Regulations, III (1973), pp. 375-86. Provisions for implementating Executive Order 11652 were published in "Directive of May 17, 1972—National Security Council Directive Governing Classification Downgrading, Declassification and Safeguarding of National Security Information," *Federal Register*, Vol. 37, No. 98, May 19, 1972.

Useful evaluations of Executive Order 11652 and its effectiveness in its first year of operations can be found in: House Report 93-221, 93rd Congress, 1st session, "Executive Classification of Information," pp. 52-87, and in Benedict Karl Zobrist III, "Reform in the Classification and Declassification of National Security Information: Nixon Executive Order 11652," *Iowa Law Review*, Vol. 59, No. 1 (October 1973), reprinted in Hearings, Subcommittee on Intergovernmental Operations and the Subcommittees on Separation of Powers and Administrative Practice and Procedure of the Committee on the Judiciary, United States Senate, 93rd Congress, 1st session on S.858, etc., April 10, 11, 12; May 8, 9, 10, 16; June 7, 8, 11, 26, 1973, Vol. III, Appendix, pp. 595-620.

6. Telephone interview with Robert B. Wells, Executive Director of the Interagency Classification Review Committee, April 19, 1976. The May 1975 progress report of the ICRC was out of print at that date, and the 1976 report was scheduled for release in June 1976. See also Interagency Classification Review Committee, "Progress Report: Implementation of Executive Order 11652 on Classification and Declassification of National Security Information and Material," April 1974.

7. Ibid.

8. Christine M. Marwick, "The Freedom of Information Act and National Security Information," *First Principles*, Vol. I, No. 3 (November 1975), p. 12.

9. Interview with Robert B. Wells.

10. Ibid.

11. Hearings, Subcommittee on Intergovernmental Relations, et al., statements of Harding F. Bancroft, executive vice-president of the *New York Times*,

pp. 157-71; statement of James B. Rhoads, Archivist of the United States, p. 325.

12. Phone interview with Beverly Zweiben, Appeals Officer of the State Department Freedom of Information Office, April 23, 1976.

13. Reprinted in Freedom of Information Act and Amendments of 1974 (P.L. 93-502), Source Book: Legislative History, Texts, and Other Documents, Joint Committee Print, Committee on Government Operations, U.S. House of Representatives, Subcommittee on Government Operations and Individual Rights and Committee on the Judiciary, U.S. Senate, Subcommittee on Administrative Practice and Procedure, 94th Congress, First Session, March 1975, p. 512.

14. P.L. 93-502.

15. Marwick, pp. 9, 11-12.

16. Interview with Beverly Zweiben.

17. Statement of Morton H. Halperin, July 25, 1974, in Hearings, Subcommittee of the Committee on Government Operations, House of Representatives, 93rd Congress, Second Session, on H.R. 12004, To Amend Section 552 of Title 5 of the United States Code (known as the Freedom of Information Act) to Provide for the Classification and Declassification of Official Information in the Interest of National Defense, July 11, 25; and August 1, 1974.

18. *Commission on the Organization of the Government for the Conduct of Foreign Policy*, U.S. Government Printing Office, June 1975, p. 201.

19. Ibid., p. 202.

20. Edward R.F. Sheehan, "Step by Step in the Middle East," *Foreign Policy* (Spring 1976), 3-70.

21. For more detailed accounts of the research on the Dominican crisis, see Carol M. Barker and Matthew H. Fox, *Classified Files: The Yellowing Pages: A Report on Scholars' Access to Government Documents*, New York: The Twentieth Century Fund, 1972, pp. 78-82. Theodore Draper, "The Classifiers of Classified Documents Are Breaking Their Own Classification Rules," *New York Times Magazine*, February 4, 1973, pp. 10-11, 38-47. Jerome Slater, Letter to the Editor, *New York Times Magazine*, May 13, 1973.

22. The distinction between documentary and empirical research is drawn from Chapter Eight of this volume, "The Legal Protection of Social Research: Criteria for Definition," by Eliot Freidson, which was most useful in clarifying my thinking on this point.

✳ *Chapter Five*

Proposed Rules on Ethics of Human Experimentation: Tensions Between the Biomedical Research Community and the United States Federal Government

Robert Levine

There are today serious conflicts in the United States between the government and the biomedical-research community on how we might best proceed to protect the rights and welfare of human subjects of experimentation. These conflicts are expressed in the activities of various branches of our state and federal governments. For example, Congress is now in the final stages of debate of a bill (H.R. 7724) which would establish a commission charged with the responsibility to, among other things, develop "appropriate guidelines for the selection of human subjects for participation in biomedical or behavioral research projects." In the courts, among the issues that are currently being tested are the rights of parents to consent to the participation of their children in research that is not designed to yield direct benefit to the children, as well as the legality of doing research on the lifeless products of legally performed abortions. The executive branch of the federal government, through the Department of Health, Education and Welfare (DHEW), is rewriting its existing policies on protection of human subjects so as to make them more strict and comprehensive and to promulgate them as rules (law) rather than as policy.[1]

To illustrate the tensions that exist I shall concentrate on discussion of the proposed DHEW rules. These are chosen because they are the most comprehensive formulation by an agency of the government of public policy in relation to human research. The reaction of the biomedical-research community is expressed as two position statements of the American Federation for Clinical Research (AFCR)[2] responding respectively to the two DHEW publications in the Federal Register. Since these statements were endorsed by unanimous votes of the governing council of the largest clinical research organization in the United States, it seems appropriate to assume that they provide valid representations of the reactions of the biomedical-research community. I shall quote from the DHEW and AFCR documents to illustrate various types of conflicts that exist. There will be no effort to provide a comprehensive presentation of all areas of difference.

SHOULD WE HAVE CONFIDENCE IN THE EXISTING SYSTEM?

One major issue raised in the current controversy is that of whether we should have confidence in the existing system to provide adequate protection of human subjects. If we proceed with the assumption that we should have confidence it would justify making no major modifications for the present, but rather continually examining the system with a view toward improving it from time to time as legitimate needs for improvement are found. On the other hand, if we assume that the existing system is inadequate there is justification for the immediate development of major modifications in the system, which—as I shall try to demonstrate—would be most costly. These costs may be expressed in terms of the enormous amounts of money that would be necessary to finance additional bureaucratic, administrative, monitoring, and reporting procedures; in terms of the negative reactions of those now engaged in biomedical research to the amount of time they would have to invest in complying with these new procedures; and in terms of the costs to the community of changing some of the major underlying assumptions of life in an academic environment. In any event, for the present we must act on assumptions; there is no clear documentation available to justify the position of either confidence or nonconfidence.

Confidence in the present system is possible only if we assume that biomedical researchers place a high value on the rights and welfare of humans in general and on the subjects of their experiments in particular. Almost all biomedical researchers are either physicians or work in close collaboration with physicians. Thus, before they embark on their research careers they are thoroughly indoctrinated in the traditions of medicine, which include a deep commitment to service to and respect for human beings. And yet we must recognize that for various reasons and under certain circumstances some investigators may become preoccupied with the scientific and methodologic aspects of their work to the extent that they may lose sight of its ethical implications.[3] Under the present system—in accord with DHEW policies—there is in each institution engaged in DHEW-sponsored research a committee that reviews proposed research for the purpose of protecting the rights and welfare of the subjects. At Yale University School of Medicine this committee is called the Human Investigation Committee (HIC). Some of the activities of the HIC will be described in detail below. Parenthetically, it should be noted that this committee was established at Yale five years before it was required by DHEW policy, and further that it reviews all research, not only that which is DHEW-sponsored.

Before an investigator may initiate any research project, he is obliged to prepare a protocol for review by the HIC. This causes him to formally shift his focus from the scientific and methodologic aspects of his work to its ethical implications. The HIC either possesses or has access to sufficient scientific expertise to assess the risks and benefits of the proposed research. It also is accustomed to thinking in terms of some of the subtle nuances of protection of subjects that often do not occur to biomedical researchers—including those who become HIC members before they are educated in the course of their HIC membership. On these bases the HIC often provides substantial assistance to the investigator in his efforts to protect the rights of subjects. The HIC assumes that the investigator conducts his research and his negotiations with subjects in accord with the final HIC-approved protocol. This assumption is based on the previously discussed assumption that biomedical researchers place a high value on the rights and welfare of humans. The existence of the HIC and formal review procedures has also resulted in a sensitization within the research community to the need to protect subjects and to observe the proprieties of informed consent. Thus, most members of the community find that there are increasingly strong peer pressures to conform.

The following description of the current activities of the HIC is offered with two main purposes in view. First, it will allow the reader to form some judgment with regard to the degree of confidence he might have in the existing system for protection of human subjects. Second, it may permit the reader to arrive at some estimate of what similar activities might cost at his own institution.

Protocols are presented to the HIC on standardized forms according to specific guidelines.[4] Among the specific categories of information requested are the following.

1. There should be a description of "past experimental or clinical findings leading to the formulation of this project." This information provides the HIC with a basis for making a judgment as to whether the state of knowledge has advanced sufficiently to justify the proposed research. For example, it may be decided that the risk-benefit ratio might be improved with the aid of further studies done in animals.

2. There should be "an estimate of the number of subjects who will be involved in the experiment as well as a statement on the population from which they will be derived." This information allows the HIC to determine what the potentials are for coercion of prospective subjects.

3. "There should be an orderly description of the intended experimental procedure as it affects the subject."

4. "List all potential hazards with some estimate (based on past experience of the investigators or of others) of their frequency, severity, and reversibility. In the event that a new drug is to be used or that an old drug is to be used for a new(non-approved) purpose it should be stated that appropriate forms have been filed with the FDA."

5. There should be specific descriptions of "the method of screening subjects and controls prior to experimentation; the means of monitoring for potential hazards; any precautions that will be taken to avoid these hazards; the point at which the experiment will be terminated if any of these hazards should occur; and the steps that will be taken to remedy the consequences of these hazardous effects. There should also be specific statements on the types of subjects that will be excluded from these studies."

The primary interest of the HIC is in the consent negotiations with the prospective subjects. The guidelines for these negotiations have been published in detail elsewhere.[5] In general, it is the policy of the HIC that an individual who is appropriately informed with regard to potential risks and benefits of and alternatives to participation in a research project should be fully empowered to decide how he will proceed. It should also be clear that the individual is not coerced to the extent that he may feel that he has lost his prerogative to exercise free choice.

There are twenty-one members of the HIC, of whom fourteen are middle- to senior-rank faculty members of the medical school. There is also a professor of law, the chaplain of the medical school, two senior administrators—one from the university and one from the hospital—and three students. These individuals meet as a committee for 1.5 hours every second week. Average activity at each of these meetings includes review of ten to twelve new protocols, two or three amendments to previously approved protocols, and annual review of ongoing protocols the number of which increases each year.

To further indicate the amount of Yale Medical School's resources committed to protection of human subjects, let us now consider the flow of a protocol from the time a research idea is conceived. First, the investigators (usually three to five) must prepare a protocol for review by the HIC. This protocol must then be endorsed by the chairman of each department in which the work is to be done (usually one or two but sometimes up to five). After appropriate endorsements are completed a sufficient number of copies (twenty-three) must be made so that each individual who will examine it will have one. These protocols are then sent to the chairman of the HIC who designates two members as primary reviewers. Primary reviewers examine the protocol to see if there are any major gaps in the information contained; if so, they attempt to contact the principal investigator so that this information will be available to the HIC at the meeting at which the protocol will be reviewed. If this is unsuccessful, it becomes necessary to table the decision to a subsequent meeting when the information is available.

After the HIC reviews the protocol the chairman writes to the principal investigator a memorandum indicating what changes will be required to obtain HIC approval. The investigator ordinarily makes these changes and approval is given at the next meeting. Sometimes it is necessary to return the protocol to the investigator two or more times for further changes. Occasionally, the investigator will feel the changes requested are inappropriate in which case he might be invited to discuss the protocol either with the entire HIC or with some of its members.

Under the proposed new DHEW rules there would be major expansions of the requirements imposed on universities for administrative, monitoring, and reporting activities. For example: "46.4 (c) Each [institutional] assurance shall contain a provision requiring the organization to give DHEW immediate notification . . . of emergent problems affecting the rights of human subjects, including adverse reactions to drugs, appliances, or other substances."[6]

To this and similar statements, the AFCR responds:

46.4 (c) This is the first of many statements that contain the implicit message that DHEW will now expect that institutions will develop mechanisms for the monitoring or policing of research activity. Examples of other statements to this effect include: 46.6 (c); the last sentence of 46.15 (a)(1); 46.18; 46.19; etc. In order to comment on these statements it is necessary to grant the validity of the assumption that the monitoring of activities by institutions—to the extent that these institutions are capable of monitoring—will have any real impact on the problems to which these new rules are addressed; we shall question the validity of this assumption in the next paragraph. Comprehensive monitoring activities will require enormous increases in the commitments of institutions to provide new positions for the people that will carry out these activities and space in which they will work. Regulations requiring monitoring activities should not be promulgated until careful studies have been completed that will determine the costs of such activities. Once the costs of these activities have been determined they can be weighed against the expected benefits. After these cost-benefit assessments have been completed, and if it is determined that monitoring activities would be of value, careful plans should be made for the implementation and financing of these activities before they are begun.

Further it is not likely that the requirements for comprehensive monitoring activities will have any real impact on the problems to which these new rules are addressed because most universities lack not only the manpower and the budget but also the expertise for their implementation. Universities have not been committed in the past to training personnel for the role of monitoring the activities of other members of the university community. Perhaps because of the basic assumptions that form the foundation of life within a university community it was never before thought necessary to develop such expertise. However, if it is determined that it is in the public interest to develop such expertise, given sufficient advance notice and support for such development, universities—which are, after all, part of the larger public—will probably find ways to contribute constructively to such development.

46.4 (c). The requirement for giving DHEW immediate notification of emergent problems affecting the rights of human subjects has been discussed in the preceding paragraphs. The requirement for immediate reporting of adverse reactions to drugs, or other substances, or appliances is not what was meant in the earlier discussion of monitoring activities. This is not inconsistent with the underlying assumptions of university life. However, it, too, is likely to greatly increase requirements for administrative personnel and activities and similarly its costs should be studied in detail and weighed against expected benefits before it is required by law. We further suggest that similar studies would be appropriate before promulgating the requirements of the following sections as they are now stated: 46.11; 46.13; 46.15 (b); and 46.16.[7]

In a subsequent draft of proposed rules DHEW establishes two additional types of review groups; ethical review boards, which would be established in each agency engaged in committing DHEW funds to support research, development, or demonstration activities involving human subjects, and protection committees in each institution that receives DHEW funds to support such activities.

46.25(a) The head of each agency shall establish an Ethical Review Board . . . to review proposals for research, development, and demonstration activities . . . to advise him or her on matters of policy concerning protection of human subjects.

(b) It shall be the function of the Board to review each proposed activity . . . and advise the agency concerning the acceptability of such activities from the standpoint of societal need and ethical considerations.[8]

This paragraph proceeds to specify functions that are already considered the responsibility of institutional primary review committees, of which the HIC is an example.

In response to this the AFCR reaffirmed its earlier position that "the new types of review groups that would be established would be extremely expensive, probably would not accomplish the purposes for which they are intended and might in fact serve to stifle research activity by imposing excessive bureaucratic obstacles to its initiation and execution."[9] The following further specific comments are offered:

We anticipate that careful studies of the activities of such boards will indicate that the interests of all concerned will be best served if they devote most of their energies to the continuing development of policy. It is likely to prove to be a needless and expensive duplication of effort for them to review each proposed activity, particularly since this will have already been accomplished by the Primary Review Committees in each institution. Another useful function of the boards would be to review the procedures proposed by Primary Review Committees to see if they are adequate. Finally, the boards could serve as courts of appeals in cases in which irreconcilable differences of opinion develop between investigators and Primary Review Committees.[10]

Although existing DHEW policies do not call for ethical review boards, review at a central level already is being performed. About three years ago we began to receive occasional letters from the Institutional Relations Branch of the Division of Research Grants of the National Institutes of Health that ethical questions had been raised on some grants submitted by faculty members of Yale University. At first these letters asked us to describe in detail the grounds on which the HIC was able to approve the described research. More recently, the letters have taken a different tone. Specifically, they have indicated that some grant applications have been refused on ethical grounds; they have not requested or even invited any response from either the HIC or the investigator.

A major factor in this problem seems to be that the sorts of information requested by DHEW in a grant request are very different from the sorts of information requested by the HIC. Investigators assume that DHEW does not want all of the details of how they will protect the rights of subjects. They assume that, since DHEW requests endorsements by the HIC, their grant applications should concentrate on the scientific aspects of their research proposals. As I mentioned earlier, the HIC sometimes finds it necessary to communicate with investigators several times to clarify their plans for protection of subjects. It would be much more difficult for centrally located Ethical Review Boards to accomplish such communications.

More recently the National Institute of Mental Health (NIMH) has begun to solicit information directly from applicants for research grants for purposes of accomplishing the same sorts of review now performed by the HIC. A form is provided, entitled Protection of Human Subjects (MH-441), which requires detailed information on the characteristics of groups of subjects to be used, the type of consent to be obtained, precautions that will be taken to safeguard confidentiality, descriptions of risks and benefits, and formal defenses of performing "nonbeneficial" research.

The proposed rules also call for the establishment of protection committees to provide further safeguards of the rights and welfare of subjects with limited capacities to consent; e.g., children, prisoners, and the mentally infirm. These protection committees are described in section 46.26 of the proposed rules.[11]

Protection committees shall be

composed of at least 5 members so selected that the committee will be competent to deal with the medical, legal, social and ethical issues involved in the activity. None of the members shall have any association with the proposed activity, and at least one-half shall have no association with any organization or individual conducting or supporting the activity. No more than one-third of the members shall be individuals engaged in research, development or demonstration activities involving human subjects.

The duties of the Protection committees

shall be to oversee: 1) The selection of subjects who may be included in the activity; 2) the monitoring of the subject's continued willingness to participate in the activity; 3) the design of procedures to permit intervention on behalf of one or more of the subjects if conditions warrant; 4) the evaluation of the reasonableness of the parents' consent and (where applicable) the subject's consent; and 5) the procedures for advising the subject and/or the parents concerning the subject's continued participation in the activity. Each subject and his or her parent or guardian will be informed of the name of a member of the Protection Committee who will be available for consultation during the activity.

The Protection Committee shall establish rules of procedure for conducting its activities, which must be reviewed by DHEW, and shall conduct its activities at convened meetings, minutes of which shall be prepared and retained.

To this the AFCR responds:

These [committees] might be of considerable value in assisting individuals with limited capacity to consent. However, it should not be required that these committees be used in all such activities. Some perspectives must be developed as to which sorts of activities require this kind of additional protection. It would be a needless waste of time and money for the Protection Committees to concern themselves with trivial interventions which bear minimum risk even in studies that are not designed to be of direct benefit to the subjects. We propose that the best way to understand the proper methods through which to design Protection Committees and to understand their functions would be to establish on an experimental basis various sorts of Protection Committees in a small number of institutions. This would be considered a research project. Protocols could be developed to get precise information on what the impact is of the existence of Protection Committees of differing compositions and with differing responsibilities.

We could also get information on the costs of these activities which would afford the possibility to develop cost-benefit assessments. Among the further questions raised by the notice in the Federal Register that will have to be resolved through such pilot studies will be the following: How can we finance the activities of members of Protection Committees who have no association with any organization or individual conducting or supporting the research activity? That is, if neither the research institution nor DHEW reimburses members of the Protection Committees for their efforts, who will? As soon as one agency or the other does take this responsibility what sorts of conflicts of interests might develop?[12]

THE ROLE OF THE RESEARCH SUBJECT

Many provisions of the DHEW proposed rules are concerned with who may decide to be a research subject, and the conditions under which he may make this decision. In some cases decision-making authority is either partially or completely transferred from the prospective subject to one of the aforementioned committees. In other cases entire categories of individuals are excluded from participation in research. (Examples of each of these displacements and exclusions will be discussed in a subsequent section.) In reflecting on these developments the AFCR states:

There is one major philosophical issue which remains to be resolved and which we do not expect can be resolved very quickly. Its resolution will have an important bearing on public policy as it will be expressed both through legislation and through regulation in the future. That is: Are we to consider the role of subject for an experiment to be a right to which all citizens are entitled unless they are deprived of this right by due process of law? Alternatively, are we to consider it a responsibility which all citizens must assume when called upon? Alternatively, we might consider it neither; it might, for example, be considered a job for which one must be compensated appropriately. In the latter case appropriate compensation might be financial or it might be the satisfaction that derives from the feeling that one has participated in the advancement of knowledge in a manner that might contribute to the welfare of one's fellow human beings.[13]

In considering this issue we may assume that agreement exists on the following points. It is in the interest of society to improve the health of people. We can enhance our ability to improve the health of people by developing better understandings of the functions of both healthy and nonhealthy people to determine, among other things, how they differ, and by developing better modalities for altering the functions of nonhealthy people so they more closely resemble those of healthy ones. These developments can be accomplished only through research. No concept developed through research done in animals can be assumed to apply to humans until it has been tested in humans. Thus it is in the interest of society to have individuals who will assume the role of experimental subject.

Most roles that are valued by our society are seen as either rights, responsibilities, or jobs. Obviously, these categories are not exclusive. In fact, most roles that we value are seen as jobs that any individual has the right to perform, provided he has the qualifications and has not been deprived of that right by due process of law.

The AFCR has taken the position that "a fully informed individual has the right to decide what experimentation he will subject himself to." In the final analysis it is the prospective subject who must decide whether the benefits to himself warrant the risks he will take. He also has the right to determine what benefits or rewards might motivate him to take certain risks. No one questions the validity of taking a risk if in return there is the potential of direct therapeutic benefit. Should we question the validity of cash payments the amounts of which are determined by customary market factors (i.e., seeing the subject role as a job)? Should we doubt that some individuals will regard the interests of the community as transcending their own? We give medals to soldiers who conspicuously risk their lives to save those of their comrades.

In the framework of our current societal practices and customs it is relatively easy to view the role of subject as a right which in some cases may also be a job. The possibility that in some circumstances it might be advantageous to consider it a duty—as we do military service—may be less apparent. This possibility and its implications particularly in relation to research on children have been discussed in detail by Alexander Capron.[14]

SOME SPECIFIC ISSUES

In this section I shall discuss several provisions of the proposed rules with which the AFCR has taken issue. This is not meant to be a comprehensive review of the provisions which have evoked anxiety or protest from the biomedical research community. Rather, it is meant to illustrate the seriousness and diversity of the problems.

One of the criteria for acceptable research proposed by DHEW is "that the risks to an individual are outweighed by the potential benefits to him or by the importance of the knowledge to be gained."[15]

To this the AFCR responds:

> This clause as it is now stated is unduly rigid and will not permit the flexibility of interpretation needed by local committees to meet the requirements of each situation that comes up. It is too rigid because it is too simple a statement of a very complex problem. For example, it does not allow a fully informed individual to consent to participate in a project in which there are risks that (in the view of some third party, e.g., a peer review group) outweigh either the potential direct benefits (to the subject) or the importance of the knowledge to be gained. In our view a fully informed individual has the right to decide what experimentation he will subject himself to. The purpose of peer review is to assure that the potential subject is fully informed so that he can make a valid decision. Further, this statement does not define either who will determine the importance of the knowledge to be gained or to whom it will be deemed important. We prefer that this statement be either expanded to accommodate the complexities of this issue or deleted entirely.[16]

Section 46.27 proposes that among the groups of children that would be excluded as potential subjects would be "the child [who] is involuntarily confined to an institutional setting pursuant to a court order, whether or not the parents and child have consented to the child's participation in the activity."[17] The AFCR observes: "Institutionalized individuals might be in the best position to serve as subjects for experiments that require continual surveillance in a controlled environment without needlessly complicating or limiting life-styles. For example, it would be much easier to do metabolic balance studies [which bear no risk to the subject] on inmates of reform schools than on freely moving adolescents who are attending public schools."[1 8]

Section 46.27 also carries a requirement that informed consent be obtained from children who are over six years of age. The AFCR agrees "with the intent of the recommendation. . . . However, since a child's understanding and comprehension may vary independently of his chronological age, we recommend that no arbitrary age be designated and that an attempt be made to involve each child in the decision at his own level of competency."

DHEW calls attention to the "ethical obligation to protect the developing fetus from avoidable harm. This obligation, along with the right of every woman to change her decision regarding abortion, requires that no experimental procedures entailing risk to the fetus be undertaken in anticipation of abortion."[1 9] Thus, "all research involving pregnant women must be reviewed by the Ethical Review Board, unless the Primary Review Committee determines that the research involves no risk to the fetus."

Since it is virtually impossible to determine in advance that there is no possibility of risk to the fetus in any significant research intervention on pregnant women, the AFCR responds:

[These regulations] would come close to destroying the entire field of fetal physiology—a field which has made great advances in recent years largely owing to the availability for study of women who are anticipating abortions. Particularly valuable are studies which begin with some experimental maneuver shortly before the abortion and which culminate in observations on the effects of this maneuver in the abortus.

Much of this very valuable research currently is supported by DHEW. We agree that every individual has the right to change his mind. However, we are aware of no data indicating that women who agree to participate in research which is justified by the fact that they are anticipating abortions often change their minds. Further information should be obtained to determine how frequently this issue actually is raised in the research environment. We must find out if there is a significant number of women who feel that they have been deprived of their options to refuse abortion because they have agreed to become subjects of studies which might have damaged the fetus.

Meanwhile, perhaps some compromise position might be reached. For example, it might be clearly worded in the consent negotiation that once a woman (and, if appropriate, the father of the fetus which she is carrying) consents to participation in a research activity which might damage the fetus she should, in effect, consider that the process of abortion will have been initiated at the time the research is begun. Truly informed consent would include the information that at the time she begins participation in the research activity she will have sacrificed the option to withdraw. Perhaps on this basis those who are uncertain about whether to proceed with the abortion will be alerted to refuse to participate as subjects in order to hold their options open. We suspect that most of these women will proceed with the abortions in any event. However, we believe that in the light of our current state of understanding of this issue, this provides a suitable compromise which not only will protect the legitimate interests of investigators who wish to contribute to the continuing development of our understanding of fetal physiology, but also will protect the interests of the parents of the fetus who, in most cases, will have made the decision to change the status of that fetus to that of abortus.[20]

The proposed new rules would proscribe artificial maintenance or termination of vital functions of the abortus for research purposes. To this the AFCR responds:

Based on the assumption that the abortus is something that is not alive it seems appropriate to proceed with the assumption that it is impossible to cause it physical or psychological pain or other discomfort and to not consider it as having any rights after it has achieved the status of abortus either spontaneously or through what public policy determines to be an appropriate human intervention. Accordingly, it seems inappropriate to proscribe the prolongation of its physiologic functions for purposes of research. Prolongation of functions such as heart beat and respiration might facilitate some important types of research without imposing any discomfort on the abortus. Similarly, termination of the heart beat or respiration would seem to be irrelevant from the point of view of the abortus (and here we are deliberately absurd in suggesting that the abortus has a point of view). Again, some important types of research can be facilitated by interventions that will abruptly stop its heart beat and/or respiration.

The ultimate disposition of the abortus should be the responsibility of those who conceived it.[21]

SUMMARY

The United States government is currently developing laws designed to protect the rights and welfare of human subjects of research. Many of the proposed new laws have elicited responses ranging from anxiety to protest from biomedical researchers. To illustrate the areas of tension that exist, this chapter quotes some specific provisions of the new rules proposed by the Department of Health, Education and Welfare and, in each case, the response of the American Federation for Clinical Research. The areas of tension are discussed in three categories.

1. Should we have confidence in the existing system to afford adequate safeguards for the research subject? Currently, no documentation is available to justify either confidence or nonconfidence. The proposed new rules seem based on the assumption of nonconfidence. Their implementation would be enormously expensive, whether expressed in terms of the amounts of money that would be necessary to finance additional bureaucratic, administrative, monitoring, and reporting procedures; in terms of the negative reactions of biomedical researchers to the amounts of time they would have to invest in compliance with new procedures; or in terms of the costs to the community of changing some of the basic assumptions of life in an academic environment. Further, there is no evidence that these new procedures would materially improve the degree of protection provided by the present system.

2. DHEW and AFCR agree that it is in the interests of society to have individuals who will assume the role of experimental subject. It would now be of value to understand the extent to which we wish to consider this role a right, a job, or a responsibility. Such an understanding would serve as a guide to those who are formulating public policy in several important respects. For example, to the extent that this role is viewed as a right, it is inappropriate to deprive qualified individuals of it without due process of law.

3. In the view of the AFCR, some specific provisions of the proposed rules are unsatisfactory, for a variety of reasons. Examples are given of provisions that are unnecessarily rigid; oversimplifications of complex problems; and exclusions of prospective subjects who either would not be put at risk or would be the major beneficiaries of some types of proposed research. One provision seems designed to protect the right of the abortus, which—as defined in the same DHEW document—is something that is not even alive.

REFERENCES

1. Department of Health, Education and Welfare, Protection of Human Subjects: Proposed Policy, *Federal Register* 38, No. 194, (October 9, 1973) 27882-85; Protection of Human Subjects, Policies and Procedures, *Federal Register* 38, No. 221, (November 16, 1973), 31738-49.

2. American Federation for Clinical Research, position statement on the proposed amendment to subtitle A of the DHEW regulations, *Clinical Research* 22 (1974), 52-54; position statement on the proposed policies and procedures for protection of human subjects, *Clinical Research* 22, (1974), 135-38.

3. B. Barber, J.J. Lally, J.L. Makarushka, and D. Sullivan, *Research on Human Subjects*, New York: Russell Sage Foundation, 1973.

4. Yale University School of Medicine, guidelines for preparation of protocols for review by the Human Investigation Committee, September 1973.

5. R.J. Levine, "Guidelines for Negotiating Informed Consent with Prospective Human Subjects of Experimentation," *Clinical Research* 22, (1974), 42-46.

6. DHEW, Protection of Human Subjects: Proposed Policy.

7. American Federation for Clinical Research, position statement on the proposed amendment to subtitle A of the DHEW regulations.

8. DHEW, Protection of Human Subjects: Policies and Procedures.

9. American Federation for Clinical Research, position statement on the proposed policies and procedures for protection of human subjects.

10. Ibid.

11. DHEW, Protection of Human Rights: Policies and Procedures.

12. American Federation for Clinical Research, position statement on the proposed policies and procedures for protection of human subjects.

13. Ibid.

14. A.M. Capron, "Legal Considerations Affecting Clinical Pharmacological Studies in Children," *Clinical Research* 21, (1973), 141-50.

15. DHEW, Protection of Human Subjects: Proposed Policy.

16. American Federation for Clinical Research, position statement on the proposed amendment to subtitle A of the DHEW regulations.

17. DHEW, Protection of Human Subjects: Policies and Procedures.

18. American Federation for Clinical Research, position statement on the proposed policies and procedures for protection of human subjects.

19. DHEW, Protection of Human Subjects: Policies and Procedures.

20. American Federation for Clinical Research, position statement on the proposed policies and procedures for protection of human subjects.

21. Ibid.

✳ *Chapter Six*

Strategies for Eliciting
and Merging Confidential
Social Research Data*

Robert F. Boruch†

INTRODUCTION

With the development of computerized record systems for
administration and of data banks for social and policy
research, many social scientists have become interested in
the possible benefits of uniting data from these (usually) different
sources of information. Indeed, a union of different archival records
on exactly the same sample of individuals appears to be a powerful
way of increasing the quality, diversity, and quantity of statistical
data available for analytical social research. Linking records from
independent federal agencies, for example, has been helpful in
appraising the accuracy and completeness of such records.[1] Similarly, epidemiological studies often require linkages among hospital and
medical service records to permit reliable documentation of the
sources and transmission of disease.[2] More generally, in sociological,
psychological, and some economic research, data merges are being
created to provide the information necessary for more realistic,
expanded models of human behavior and for better evaluation of
social programs.[3]

*Supported by NSF Grants G129843 and GS320-73X. Professors Eli Ruben-
stein, Donald T. Campbell, and Lance Hoffman were generous in providing
advice on earlier drafts of the paper. However, views expressed here do not
necessarily reflect the views of the sponsoring agency or of these individuals.

†Director of the Division of Methodology and Evaluation Research (Psychology Department) at Northwestern University, Evanston, Illinois.

Reprinted from *Policy Sciences* (1972), Vol. 3, No. 2, pp. 275-297. with
permission of Elsevier Publishing Company, Amsterdam.

A more recent, perhaps belated, development has been the researcher's recognition that social and legal constraints on access to archival data can inhibit and prevent useful data unions. Such formal constraints are perhaps exemplified by Federal regulations against disclosure of identifiable records, e.g., the U.S. Census Bureau,[4] Social Security Administration,[5] and Internal Revenue Service restrictions. Similar policy can also prevent data unions at the local level; the Russell Sage Foundation Guidelines,[6] for example, suggest that pupils' school records not be released to anyone, including researchers, for any purpose, except under fairly restrictive conditions.

OBJECTIVES

Regarding such constraints as legitimate, but assuming that merged data can have some genuine research benefits, what strategies might the social scientist employ in order to conduct research on a union of data? The primary objective of this chapter is to examine, appraise, and extend certain techniques that appear to answer this question. The techniques and the models on which they are based permit the researcher to merge his own records with archival data, and to merge the data from independent agencies without violating formal regulations or promises of confidentiality which pertain to the individuals on whom records are maintained.

Three related classes of models are developed here; the effectiveness of each depends, in part, on cryptographic encoding of statistical data, of identifiers, or of both these portions of each archival record. (Cryptographic encoding is defined here as the general process of creating and substituting arbitrary characters (or code groups) for the characters within an archival record.) The first class, the "insulated" data bank model, is quite simple and involves a single encode-decode operation on statistical data. In the second class, a brokerage agency is introduced to avoid certain problems in the first class of models and to merge the data. The third class requires a broker to maintain code linkage systems for merging data and updating archival information. The following discussion is divided into three major sections corresponding to this taxonomy of models. Within each section, variations on the particular model are discussed and the model's benefits and corruptibility are examined. Although the context of discussion is typically computerized record systems, the examples demonstrate that the models can be applied to noncomputerized systems in a variety of organizational environments.

THE INSULATED DATA BANK CONCEPT

During 1966, Schwartz and Orleans[7] designed a true field experiment to appraise the effect of threats of legal reprisal and of appeals to moral conscience on the completeness of income-tax reporting. To do the experiment, the researchers needed a mechanism for merging their own data on a sample of individuals with Internal Revenue Service records on the same individuals without compromising their promise to participants that the information supplied by the latter would remain confidential, and without violating IRS regulations on disclosure. Figure 6-1 illustrates a generalization of the strategy devised by Schwartz to merge the data under these conditions. For the sake of clarity suppose that the researchers are represented by Agency A in the diagram; their file of data on the individuals in the experiment are symbolized by AI, where A indicates (say) membership in an experimental or control group and I is a personal identifier. Similarly, B represents the archival agency (the IRS) and BI symbolizes identifiable income tax records.

The model in Figure 6-1 implies that to accomplish the merge the researchers must first cryptographically encode the statistical portions of each record in their file, producing a new file A'I, which is then transmitted to the archival agency. The agency then matches files A'I and BI, basing the match on clear identifiers (I) appearing in each record. Upon completion of the merge, identifiers are deleted

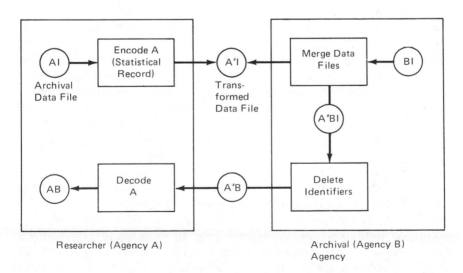

Figure 6-1. Insulated Data Bank

and the file labeled A'B is returned to the researchers for decoding, editing, and analysis.

Under rigorous application of the model the researchers gain raw statistical data (i.e., devoid of identifiers) but never have or require direct access to identifiable records controlled by the archival agency. The archival agency, on the other hand, never gains knowledge of the attributes described by file AI, in accordance with the researcher's original promise to maintain the confidentiality of those data. In addition to the application cited above, the strategy has been used successfully in evaluative studies of education[8] and of manpower training programs,[9] which involve data from restricted archival sources. The model is not completely free from the possibility of corruption, however. Since corruptibility depends, in part, on the situation to which the model is applied, variations on the basic model are discussed in the next section; corruptibility and more secure extensions of the model are then examined.

Variations on the Model

One can examine at least three useful variants on this model by manipulating the identity of Agency B and the flow of information implied by the model. Assuming that Agency A represents a single researcher initiating the merge of data, we can consider Agency B as a single archival agency or researcher, as several independent archival agencies, and finally as the research subject.

Single Institution/Single Researcher.   This variation conforms, of course, to the example given above, but some additional remarks on the model's utility are justified.

Consider, for example, the situation in which independent researchers A and B obtain different data on the same individuals. Typically, both social scientists will promise the respondent that his response will be confidential. Aside from fostering good response rate, such a promise fulfills a mandatory requirement in some federally sponsored research that the rights of subjects in social research be fully recognized. The researchers, however, may wish to furnish identified data to a professional colleague for research purposes, with an informal agreement that the colleague must not disclose identified records. Should the respondent, his representatives, or the sponsoring agency view such an exchange as a breach of confidentiality, then the insulated data bank concept may help to ameliorate ethical problems. Since no interpretable, identified records are exchanged, the subjects' reports are anonymous with respect to anyone but the researcher to whom he supplied the information.

More subtle uses of the insulated data bank model concern institutional records which legitimately fall into the category of public information or which are treated more ambiguously as "pseudo-public" records. In either case, the researcher may be confronted with bona fide legal impediments to accessing identifiable information, and these difficulties may be exacerbated by the archival agency's arbitrary interpretation of regulations or statutes. The publicly supported United Planning Organization,[10] for example, has established an "information trust" for its archival data to avoid disclosing identifiable records to any persons outside the agency. Although the trust's legal tenability has been criticized,[11] a trust could be sufficient to prevent outside researchers' appraising the quality of the data and merging the UPO data with other information for the sake of policy research. In this situation, the model might be regarded as an expedient and economical device for accomplishing research objectives.

Multiple Institution Case. A schematic diagram, representing the multiple-institution variant of the mutually insulated data bank model, is presented in Figure 6-2. It should be evident that logistical problems become much more complex when more than one separate institution is involved with Agency A in merge operations. Specifically, Agency A must encode its data AI (AI becomes A'I). Agency B must merge A'I with BI, encode the data file A'BI, and transmit the encoded file A'B'I to Agency C. Encoding of Files AI and BI is necessary to prevent personnel at Agency C from interrogating identifiable records. File CI is merged with the encoded data by Agency C and identifiers are removed and the resulting file (A'B'C) is returned to Agency B for partial decoding. After decoding the B' portion of the file, Agency B returns File A'BC to Agency A for further decoding, editing, and analysis.

One of the appealing features of this variant is that it provides a kind of primitive resolution to the problems raised by the proposal for a National Data Center.[12] Rather than maintain all data under its own auspices as planned, the National Data Center could, for example, solicit and merge identifiable information from both the U.S. Census Bureau and the Internal Revenue Service without violating their respective rules for confidentiality, by using the model. Similar variations are possible in the private research sector. For example, the American Council on Education and the American College Testing Service collect identifiable research information, under a promise of confidentiality, from over 300,000 students annually. Insofar as the samples overlap with one another, applica-

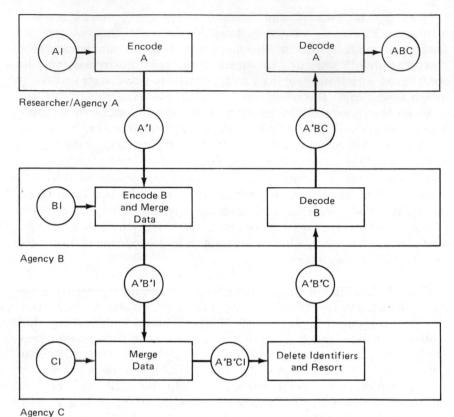

Figure 6-2. Multi-institutional Variant of Insulated Data Bank

tion of the insulated data bank model may help considerably to eliminate redundancy in elicited information, to appraise the credibility of the data, and to extend the time series available for analysis, all without compromising agreements about disclosure of individual records.

Respondent. Now consider the situation in which the respondent is presumed to have some information about himself which is of interest to the researcher; information which must be linked with data previously obtained from the respondent in order to maximize its utility. Usually, it is quite simple to elicit identifiable information from a respondent and to later merge it with prior information held by the researcher.

The insulated data bank model may be useful, however, when identifiable information is very sensitive, e.g., when truthful response to the inquiry could result in social or legal action against the respondent. In the American Council on Education's Study of Campus Unrest, for example, information on student protest activities was linked directly from college students, and this information was to be linked with other information (on the same students) available in the ACE data bank.[13] Such a linkage would provide a substantial base for understanding the statistical relations between protest activity and the previous interests and achievements of students. But the sensitivity of the data suggests that some mechanism must be developed for eliminating the possibility that the data be used for nonresearch purposes.

One strategy for coping with legal threats to data in this situation is based on the insulated data bank model, with the respondent acting as Agency B. The researcher consolidates his prior information on an individual, punches the data into, say, a single IBM card, and provides it to the respondent. This information would be encoded if there was reason to expect clear information to influence the individual's decision to respond or the substance of his response, or if there is some risk of disclosure to third parties during the process of punching cards and transmitting them to the respondent. One column of the card remains blank, but it is perforated to allow the respondent himself to punch out a "1" if, for example, he has participated in a protest and an "0" if he has not. By punching his response in the specified column, and by punching all our perforations in the identifier columns, the respondent effectively merges his own data file with the researcher's, while maintaining his anonymity. The cycle implied in the model is completed when each member of the respondent group returns his card to the researcher. (In order to appraise validity of a sample in which subjects volunteer to respond, a postcard containing only an identifier can be provided to each subject. Return of the postcard by the subject indicates that he has returned his response under separate cover.)

Note that, if the encode-decode operation is eliminated from this paradigm, the model is identical to the classical survey scheme in which questionnaires are mailed to identified individuals in a sample and returned anonymously by the same individuals.

Corruptibility of the Insulated Data Bank Model

When used judiciously, the model is attractive in several respects. Its logical basis, composition, and process are all quite simple; yet as we have seen it, it can be imposed on a variety of situations requiring a merge of data. Furthermore, the objectives and the steps for implementing the model are clear enough to facilitate communication with the individual who expresses a reasonable apprehension about the union of data files.

On the other hand, the model has two major weaknesses that might undermine and perhaps destroy its utility. The first weakness is a logistical one: few agencies or individuals who are placed in the role of Agency B may be capable of accurate match-merge operations even when the volume of data is small. Merging large data files can be very expensive, particularly when search and match strategies, whether computerized or manual, are inefficient.[14] When the respondent plays the role of Agency B, implementing the model may be very difficult because of his resistance or indifference to the research, communications problems between researcher and respondent, and so forth.

The second weakness involves possible corruption of the model by Agecy A or Agency B. When the encoding transform is a good one, it is impossible for Agency B to corrupt the system unless it had access to the decipher key or can infer the contents of File AI. I will assume that any such access can be prevented by the usual physical safeguards and personnel checks; otherwise there is no real justification for encoding. Petersen and Turn[15] describe and evaluate these safeguards. Agency A (the researcher), on the other hand, may corrupt the model in at least two ways: encoding duplicate identifiers, and merging data sequentially. Using the first corruption method, Agency A duplicates identifiers in each record, producing a File AII. Then, Data Set A and one set of identifiers are encoded, producing Data File $A'I'I$. The deletion of I after match-merging by Agency B is specious, since Agency A can decipher the resultant Data file, $A'I'B$, and acquire identifiable merged records.

An alternative method of corruption involves the use of attribute data as partial identifiers. If each individual's record is *completely* unique, the statistical record itself constitutes an identifier. Again, Agency B's deletion of interpretable identifiers after the match-merge process by Agency B is specious; Agency A's duplicate file of AI can be used with the unique statistical records to disclose the association between the formal identifiers (I) and elements from Data File B. A variant on this method of corruption is also possible through sequential match-merge operations. That is, one can elicit sequential merges of data, using different elements in the B file to construct a dossier on specific individuals in the AI file. Although time-consuming, this "twenty questions" strategem is feasible, and well documented;[16] the difficulty of detecting accidental disclosure stemming from this strategy is described by Miller[17] for the case of Census data.

Considering these potential weaknesses—logistical requirements and corruptibility—how can the social scientist eliminate or minimize risks attached to its use? One obvious device for ameliorating the logistical problems is shifting merge responsibility to an independent brokerage agency; this is discussed in the section on brokerage models below. The more difficult task of developing mechanisms to inhibit and eliminate threats of corruption are discussed in the next section.

More Secure Versions of the Insulated Data Bank Model

Several mechanisms to cope with the possibility of Agency A's subverting the model will be considered here: trust and/or licensing, monitoring the merge process, inoculating files with error, and limiting Agency A's access to raw data files.

Trust or Licensing. The respondent's trust in the social researcher has always been an important ingredient in the researcher's direct acquisition of social data. In the context of the insulated data model, either simple trust or formal recognition of trust by Agency B's licensing the researcher's conduct may be quite justified, especially if the participating agencies and the subjects of records can agree to criteria for trustworthiness. The justification may be strengthened considerably if there is some formal mechanism for taking punitive action against Agency A should the model be subverted. In the simple trust relationship, for example, the threat of no further access to data may be sufficient to offset any benefits that might accrue to the researcher's corrupting the model. Licensing by employment, as used by the Census Bureau for legally achieving data merges, carries the threat of legal sanction against individuals who violate rules against disclosure of identifiable information.[18]

Although we admit that the integrity of Agency A is one kind of safeguard against corruption, we must also observe that a meaningful appraisal of integrity and the development of licensing methods is often difficult and time consuming. Moreover, if we can capitalize on other safeguards, we may be able to eliminate the need to rely solely on the apparent integrity of Agency A.

Monitors. Another strategy for inhibiting corruption of the kinds described earlier involves the use of monitors during the merge process. Agency B might continuously observe the conduct of the merge and examine the physical contents of data files supplied by Agency A for the merge. The examination of contents must be focused on detecting uniqueness of each and every statistical record and on sequential merges so as to prevent match-merges of statistical records which are potentially identifiable. Monitoring, however, may be too expensive, too time consuming, or too weak to detect and prevent all but obvious attempts to corrupt the model. In fact, it would be difficult, if not impossible, for a monitor to detect the presence of encoded identifiers (i.e., Data File A'I'I supplied by Agency A) if sophisticated enciphering techniques are used.

Error Inoculation.   An alternative safeguard can be employed by either Agency A or Agency B to minimize the utility of potentially identifiable records in this model. They may simply inoculate random errors into the records on that copy of File BI which is involved in the merge. It is possible to control the statistical properties of the random error which is introduced and, although the integrity of any particular record is undermined, the statistical condensations of the merged (imperfect) data can frequently be corrected for errors using common mathematical techniques. The strategy has not been tested adequately in large-scale operations and it is possible that, by inoculating error, subtle characteristics of the data will be rendered inaccessible to even the most sophisticated statistical analysis. But the technique's theoretical underpinnings appear to have been sufficiently well developed to permit application in the data merge situation as well as in direct interviews.[19]

Limiting Data Access.   Given the limitations of error inoculation, of monitoring, and of licensing, one might extend the original model by limiting Agency A's access to raw individual records.

Such an extension is illustrated in Figure 6-3. This new model implies that Agency B will not only match-merge the data, but also furnish a statistical summary rather than raw records to Agency A. Agency A must specify, prior to merging data, all the summaries necessary for its own analysis of the merged data.[a] Providing statistical summaries reduces the potential for corruption (by encoding identifiers or by de facto statistical identifiers) when certain conditions are met. The conditions are simple and depend on the kind of data condensation which is prescribed and developed.

---

[a]In order to summarize data adequately, Agency B would normally use existing computer programs for calculated measures of central tendency, dispersion, and associational statistics such as covariance matrices. If commonly available programs are inadequate, and more sophisticated ones cannot be supplied by Agency A, then data might be micro-aggregated instead. That is, very small groups of individuals are specified and the average observations on these groups, rather than on single individuals, are furnished to Agency A. Although micro-aggregation techniques are still primitive, they are generating researchers' interest partly because they are a convenient device for preserving anonymity of records disseminated from archival systems.[21]

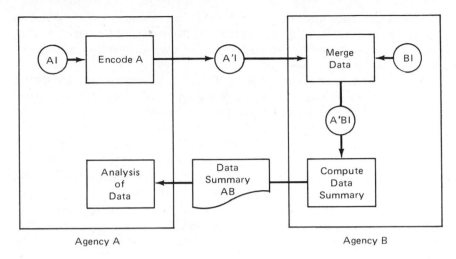

Figure 6-3. Extended Version of Insulated Data Bank Model

Frequency distributions, cross-tabulations, and other statistics can be produced under the constraint that the observed frequencies within all cells be above a certain number; Agency B would, for example, require that all statistics be based on at least thirty observations within any particular group. Monitoring may still be necessary to detect and prevent the sequential method of corruption when frequencies, counts, or cross-tabs are solicited periodically by Agency A.

When statistical summaries, rather than raw data, are furnished to Agency A, cryptographic encoding of AI takes on a different cast. The classic encoding mechanisms change the character and mathematical properties of the data completely and statistics based on such data may be meaningless. In lieu of encoding, the researcher can exploit common statistical transforms[20] of data or simple linear functions of the actual data can be employed; the statistical transformations may, in any event, be essential for adequate analysis of the data. Both statistical and linear transforms disguise rather than cryptographically encode data. However, this strategy ought to be sufficient to inhibit overt interrogation or duplication of data files by the broker, Agency B, and Agency A when each of these groups monitors the merge process.

BROKERAGE MODELS

In this section, a brokerage agency, whose function is to match-merge data is incorporated into the formal structure of earlier models. Variations on the brokerage model are also discussed. The possibility of corrupting the system is treated only briefly in the context of each variation, since the earlier remarks on the subject are also relevant to this model.

The simplest brokerage model, illustrated in Figure 6-4, is a direct extension of the insulated data bank model, and contains most of the same elements and flows of information. In the model, Data File AI is generated by Agency A, and the statistical portions of each record are encoded (i.e. AI becomes A'I. Similarly, Agency B generates encoded the Data File B'I using a different enciphering algorithm. The two resultant files, A'I and B'I, are match-merged by the broker, based on the unique identification portion of each record (I). Encoding is intended to protect the files against interrogation by the broker during the merge process. Following the match-merge operation, all identifiers are deleted and Data File A'B' is returned to

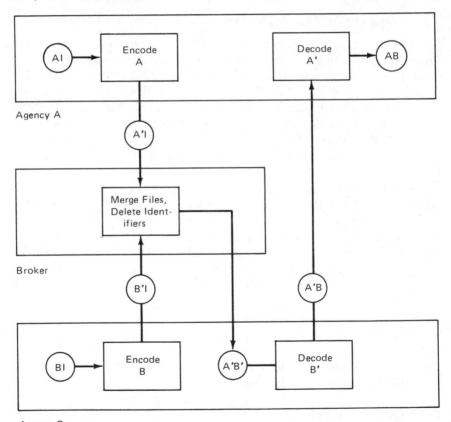

Figure 6-4. Brokerage Model

Agency B for decoding. This partially decoded file, A'B, is then sent to Agency A for decoding, editing, and analysis.

By moving responsibility for match-merging from Agency B to the broker, we have reduced some of Agency B's obligations, thereby ameliorating a disadvantage of the models discussed above. A decoding operation has been added to Agency B's responsibility (i.e. B' to B) and if Agency B considers this to be an unwarranted imposition, Agency A can be provided with the decipher code for decoding the B' sections of the merged file.

Although one of Agency B's obligations has been eliminated by having the broker merge the data, and the encoded data file is secure against interrogation by the broker, the potential for corruption of the system by Agency A still has not been reduced. If trust, licensing arrangements, or other mechanisms appear to be insufficient for assuring that files will not be corrupted by Agency A, then an alternative model can be used. This model, given by Figure 6-5, requires Agency B to summarize the data according to a form specified a priori by Agency A, and to merge the files. Data summaries might include averages, cross-tabulations, etc. As in the extended version of the insulated data bank model, monitoring is necessary to prevent use of the twenty-questions stratagem in corrupting the system. Inoculating records with small amounts of random error with known parameters will help to minimize the utility of identifiable records to the broker as well as to each agency should the records actually be somehow decoded. Perhaps the best method of further inhibiting the broker's ability to interrogate identifiable records is to cryptographically encode the *identifiers* in each file, using a unique encoding scheme developed jointly by Agency A and Agency B.

Variations on the Brokerage Models

Three variants on the brokerage model are considered here: a "neutral agency," the respondent, and the researcher, each considered as the broker in the system.

Neutral Agency. At times, it may be desirable for Agencies A and B to engage some neutral agency to merge their files. "Neutral" here might be defined as a condition of having no apparent interest or need to interrogate identifiable data; or neutrality may be specified as legal immunity from any outside penetration of identified records. For example, Edgar Dunn and others[22] have suggested that the Census Bureau or a similar specially created federal agency be used to fulfill a similar brokerage role so as to merge federal records for

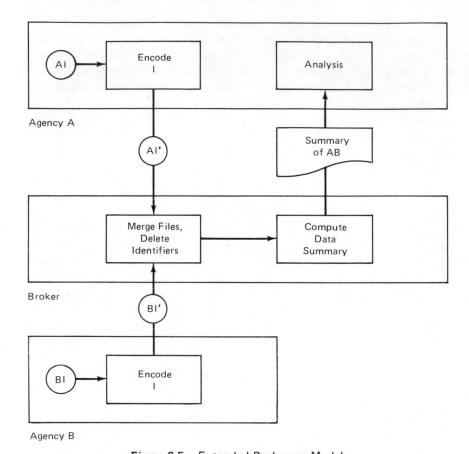

Figure 6-5.   Extended Brokerage Model

research purposes. Similarly, if Agencies A andB want to merge files which concern sensitive but well-defined research areas such as alcohol abuse, then data merges might be conducted under the auspices of the National Institute for Alcohol Abuse and Alcoholism (Public Law 91-616). In both cases, statutory testimonial privilege would render the records in their possession immune from legal interrogation.

One obvious problem in this context is that federal agencies are unlikely to regard themselves as brokers for social scientists who wish to merge data. Unless legislation or executive direction specifies that this activity is consistent with their missions, the agencies will probably not be able to muster the logistical support necessary for implementing the models. Rather than rely on governmental agencies, we may then choose a commercial service group or accounting firm to act as broker under contractual agreements to maintain the confidentiality of the data. When the identifiers and statistical data are encoded by Agencies A and B and when there is strict monitoring of the merge process (with safeguards against secret reproduction of files, merged or otherwise), there appears to be no critical problem in using such an agency. Such agencies, of course, cannot furnish statutory protection for the files they maintain and process.

Respondent. Suppose that Agencies A and B, be they independent researchers or institutions, cannot agree on a choice of institutional broker. Their unwillingness to do so may be caused by general distrust of the candidates for brokerage, by their suspicion of the model, or by a reluctance to incur expenses implied by the brokerage model. Under these conditions, the individual on whom records are maintained might substitute as a broker. He can merge data sets that are furnished to him independently by Agencies A and B; following the merge he may delete identifiers and return the documents to Agency A. This strategy may be particularly adaptable to institutional settings such as hospitals, prison systems, colleges, etc., in which the process of eliciting the merged data can be controlled well.

In less controllable situations, using the respondent as a broker is inferior to other strategies to the extent that nonresponse rate is liable to be high and logistical problems serious. Moreover, any of the corruption strategies mentioned in connection with the insulated data bank model are applicable in this case. This weakness suggests that the use of a respondent-as-broker strategy does not then appear to be a good one unless there is some justification (e.g. trust or licensing) for believing that Agency A is not interested in obtaining identifiable records.

Researcher. Using the researcher as broker requires a slightly different interpretation of the information exchanges described earlier. Specifically, the symbols for Agency A and Agency B represent the respondent at two different points in time. Rather than encoding statistical portions of the record, each individual in the sample encodes his identification uniquely and in accordance with his own enciphering technique. The respondent's consistent use of this alias at points A and B in time permits the researcher, acting as broker, to match-merge data obtained from the respondent at times A and B. (Note that flow lines in the diagrams must be adjusted so that merge, summarization, and analysis of results are conducted under the auspices of the researcher.) Aliases can be constructed systematically using a variety of instructions and, so long as the researcher lacks the ability to link aliases with true identification, the anonymity of the respondent is protected. Numeric aliases, created by the subject on the basis of prescribed formula, have been used by Rossi et al.[23] in longitudinal drug studies of the college population. Experience with studies of students' political activity suggest that arbitrary aliases created by subjects themselves may function at least as well as numerical aliases.[24]

CODE-LINKAGE SYSTEMS

In some research efforts, code linkages between different archival data files have been created and are maintained indefinitely to permit merges and updating of data. A simplified form of code linkage system, presented in Figure 6-6, specifies the basic objectives and composition of the system. Since the justification for more elaborate

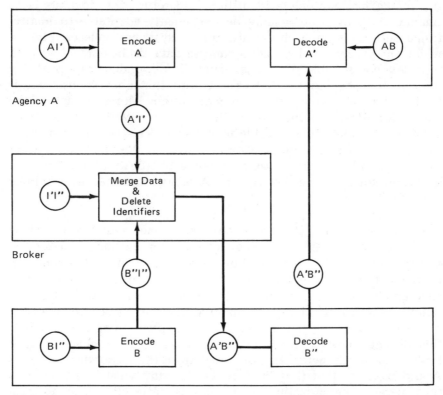

Figure 6-6. Simplified Code-Linkage Model

models depends, in large measure, on their particular research application, two such models—the Manniche-Hayes and the ACE Link File Systems—are discussed in detail following description of this elementary one.

The simplest code-linkage system is characterized by three basic elements: two agencies each maintaining independent, identifiable data on the same persons, and a broker that is responsible for maintaining the code linkage. To merge data, Agency A encodes the statistical portion of its records using one encryption scheme (A becomes A'); identifying information has at some previous time been encoded using a different encryption scheme (I becomes I'). Similarly, Agency B encodes the statistical portion of each record in its own file. Identifiers in this file, as in File AI, have been encoded previously but using an encoding scheme which differs from that used by Agency A (I in File BI is then coded as I''). The two resulting data files, A'I' and B''I'', are transmitted to the broker, which then merges the data based on its knowledge of the linkage between coded identifiers (i.e. I'I''). Encoded identifiers, I' and I'', are deleted and the merged Data File A'B'' is returned first to Agency B for decoding and then to Agency A for further decoding and analysis.

This model exhibits several potential benefits over preceding models. Protecting the records against corruption by Agency A is unnecessary under optimal operation of the model, since the model specifies that Agency A maintains only encoded identifiers in its own statistical record. The likelihood that the broker can obtain and decipher both encoded records and encoded identifiers is low, if the code linkage is maintained in a very secure environment (free from third-party interrogation, legal or otherwise). So far, however, the actual mechanism for generating the encoded identifiers and code linkages has not been described. Because this mechanism is crucial to the integrity of the model and to its distinctiveness relative to those described earlier, the two published descriptions of code-linkage use are examined below with special regard for the method of generating code linkages and the corruptibility of models implied by each description.

Manniche-Hayes System

A *generalized* form of the original Manniche-Hayes[25] strategy is illustrated in Figure 6-7. In the original application, the purpose of the strategy was to enable the researchers to obtain data from confidential university records and to obtain other data from students on whom the records were kept, without violating college

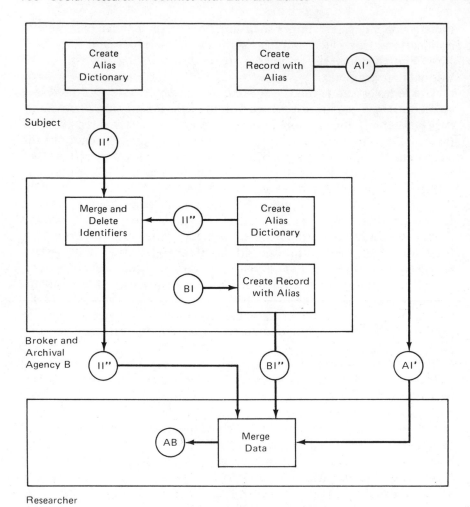

Figure 6-7. Manniche-Hayes Code-Linkage System

regulations on disclosure and without eliciting any identifiable information directly from students. An important corollary objective was to elicit and match-merge data without coming into possession of any identifiable records whatsoever, and without allowing any other agency to have access to identifiable information elicited directly from students. The process symbolized by Figure 6-7 has the following characteristics. The broker must be an individual with access to the archival records, e.g. a college registrar in the current example. He first consolidates all relevant identifiable records, BI, from the archive. Then he encodes the identifiers in this file and supplies the resulting file, BI″, to the researcher. He also creates and maintains a dictionary to catalogue each clear identifier with each encoded identifier: II″.

In effect, the subjects of research also create a data file with encoded identifiers and a dictionary. Each subject creates an alias or other arbitrarily encoded identifier and attaches it to a record of information elicited by the researcher, e.g. questions about drug usage. Each subject also creates an elemental dictionary linking his true identifier with the alias. The subject's responses, identified only by alias (AI′), are supplied to the researcher, while each elemental dictionary (II′) is supplied to the broker.

The broker, having dictionary II″ (created by him) and dictionary II′ (created by subjects), match-merges these on the basis of the clear identifiers (I) appearing in both dictionaries. After deleting identifiers he furnishes this code-linkage file, I′I″, to the researcher. Given Data File BI″ from the archive, Data File AI′ from the subjects, and the code linkage between them, File I′I″, the researcher can merge the files easily and analyze the resultant file, AB, at his convenience.

This model, therefore, permits the researcher to elicit information directly from a sample of individuals and from an archival source, and to match-merge the information without having access to identifiable data from either source. The model is flexible but, in some cases, corruptible; variations on the model and corruptibility are discussed next.

Variations on the Manniche-Hayes Model. One of the interesting variations on the model is composed of a researcher and broker as just described, but it includes a second archival agency (or researcher), instead of the respondent, as another source of research information. So defined, the model constitutes an alternative to some of the variations on the insulated data bank or the brokerage models. For example, the researcher might simply ask for specific data from both archives on a random sample of individuals selected by one of the archival agencies. He would have no need to know the identification of each individual if the sampling was random, the match-merge accurate, and the data pertinent to his research requirements. The model then represents one solution to the problem of merging data from service-oriented data banks which may not have the capability for constructing summaries of the data but which do want to minimize the likelihood of the researcher's corrupting the merge process.

The model is particularly relevant to merges of archival records on individuals who might object to their being identified as having an institutional record, even though the identification is disassociated from statistical information. For example, former mental patients may (and do) register objections to an evaluation researcher's knowing their names and the fact that they have been patients, even though the researcher has no other information. Similarly, individuals may prefer not to have an outside researcher know that they have dealt with a particular bank, loan company, or political group. The insulated data bank model, its extensions, and the brokerage models are all insufficient for handling this situation, since they do require that the researcher have some clear identification of each in his sample. Because the broker in the code-linkage model can elicit information on behalf of the researcher without actually handling such information or revealing identifiers to the researcher, the scheme can be applied to situations in which identification itself constitutes a sensitive record.

Corruptibility of the Model. Because the model never involves a flow of data originating from the research agency, the researcher has no opportunity to corrupt the scheme by encoding identifiers. In fact, if there is no listing of research subjects, as would be the case in match-merges of random samples from two data archives or in a merge that involes the broker's eliciting information on behalf of the researcher, it would be difficult, if not impossible, to use the twenty-questions stratagem to construct identifiable information on subjects.

Suppose, however, that the merge must be based on a complete population defined by the researcher and whose membership may be known, in whole or in part, to the researcher. One might elicit state prison records as well as information directly from inmates under the model; knowing the identities of each member of the population, and having some public information on these members, it would be an easy matter to impute the identifiers associated with each record. It is doubtful that monitoring of the raw data will eliminate or help reduce this possibility. Aside from simple trust or licensing, only two alternatives seem to be reasonable. The broker may inoculate raw records with random error to reduce the likelihood of correct imputation, or another agency might be introduced into the system. This agency would be monitored by representatives of Agencies A and B and of the researcher group to assure that no one systematically reviewed the records for the purpose of building identified dossiers. This agency would be responsible for collecting the records, match-merging them, and supplying summary data (rather than raw records) to the researcher.

ACE Link File System

This variation on the code-linkage model was created in direct response to public and professional apprehension about maintaining identifiable records in a long-term educational research program at the American Council on Education.[26] Illustrated in Figure 6-8, the ACE Link File System employs a foreign broker to maintain the code linkage file ($I'I''$). Data File AI represents information gathered by the research agency at Time 1, while information corresponding to Data File BI is collected and consolidated at a second later point in time. The information in this case concerns demographic characteristics, achievements, political attitudes and activities, and other data on over one million college students.

File AI'' is constructed at Time 1 by replacing true identifiers (I) with a set of encoded identifiers. Two dictionaries are then constructed by the research agency. One dictionary, II', catalogues the association between clear identifiers (I) and a second set of encoded identifiers (I'), where the encryption scheme for this second set differs from that used in the first set. Both File AI' and dictionary II' are maintained by A.C.E. The second dictionary consists of the linkage between the two sets of encoded identifiers ($I'I''$); it is constructed by the research agency but is sent to the broker for storage and use by the broker alone. The research agency then holds only nonidentifiable data in its AI'' file and a dictionary II' for use in later merges of data.

Merging of File AI'' with data gathered later, File BI, involves three stages. The research agency first replaces clear identifiers in File BI with encoded identifiers from the II' dictionary. The dictionary is destroyed and the new file, BI', is sent to the broker. The broker then replaces the set of identifiers (I') in this file with a new set from its dictionary, $I'II''$. The resulting file, BI'', is returned to the research agency, where it is merged with file AI'' on the basis of the identifier common to both files (I'').

When the model is rigorously adhered to, the Link File System demonstrates some important ways for preventing interrogation of identifiable records during the merge process. The process of merging AI' with BI'' is free from threat of the broker's penetration, since only encoded identifiers in File AI' are supplied to the broker. The data-merge process appears to be safe, the researchers themselves not being able to decipher the encoded identifiers in AI'' and BI'' because they no longer have the decipher key. A final benefit is that Data File BI'' and succeeding data files are maintained without risk of extralegal or legal interrogation of files. True identifiers are legally inaccessible, since (in the ACE case) the broker is a foreign agency

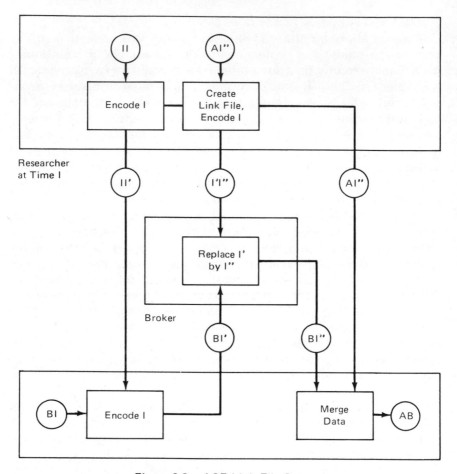

Figure 6-8. ACE Link File System

and the agreement between broker and researchers specifies that the linkage be kept secret and secure, even from the researchers themselves.

Variations on the ACE Link File System. The ACE System was developed mainly to prevent any legal or extralegal interrogation of data files that had to be updated periodically. This limitation in objectives does not permit one to vary participating agencies easily. In fact, the only variation that seems to be reasonable is one in which the research agency elicits data from other archival agencies rather than directly from subject. But in this case, the model may be less desirable than, say, the generalization of the Manniche-Hayes model because of its complexity and its potential for corruptibility.

Corruptibility of the Link File System.   This model is vulnerable to some of the same corruption strategies mentioned in the context of the insulated data bank and the brokerage models. The problems described below are based on the writer's own perceptions, and on two very professional critiques by Dr. Rein Turn of Rand Corporation and Dr. Lance Hoffman of the University of California at Berkeley (both personal communications).

Suppose we first examine the possibility of corruption of the system by members of the research agency. First, there is no real guarantee that the agency actually destroys copies of Files BI or the code linkage I'II''; given the File AI and II', of course, completely identifiable records (of the form ABI) can be constructed, subverting the purpose of the system. Actually, covert duplication and maintenance of Files BI and I'I'' by a member of the research agency or the failure to destroy original files at the appropriate time is not really necessary to permit later interrogation of identifiable records. One need only construct a covertly encoded identifier in each record of File BI'', a simple extension of a corruption strategy mentioned in connection with earlier models.

The brokerage agency constitutes a second potentially weak element in the system. If the broker has access to the list of individuals whose records are maintained, it may then construct its own file of commonly available data about those individuals. Given these data, its copy of Data File BI', and the documentation for the file, the broker may be able to interrogate the file and build its own dossiers, using the twenty-questions stratagem. One convenient way to ameliorate this difficulty has been suggested by Lance Hoffman: the researchers must encode the statistical position of each record (that is B is transformed to B''), using a unique encoding scheme which is unavailable to the broker.

Dr. Turn has emphasized the weaknesses of foreign as opposed to domestic maintenance of link files. He contends that one objective of the system—keeping link files secure from legal penetration—would not be met if, for example, foreign courts submitted quite readily to our government's requesting the linkges. Formal international negotiations may be quite unnecessary if acquisition and disclosure of link files is informally interpreted and accomplished as an amicable understanding between governments. If the foreign agency chooses not to abide by its contract to maintain the link file (or if it decides to sell the information), then the system's functional utility is destroyed. Moreover, successful prosecution of the broker may be so difficult and time consuming that the system's utility would be impaired considerably, if not destroyed entirely.

These kinds of weaknesses in brokerage are improbable (although still possible) if the broker is selected carefully, and if there are some external guarantees of adherence to the model. In the ACE system, one such guarantee is the ACE agreement to provide exactly the same link file services to researchers at the foreign agency. If the foreign broker ignores its own responsibility toward ACE, then presumably, ACE can make similar reprisals. Such a potentially destructive countermeasure is not particularly appealing, but it may be a useful mechanism for deterring violations of formal contract or informal agreements.

SUMMARY AND DISCUSSION

Each of the strategies described here—the insulated data bank concept, the brokerage models, and code-linkage system—permit the social researcher to unite his own data on individuals with other archival data on the same individuals, without violating sociolegal prohibitions against disclosure of archival records and, furthermore, without violating promises of data confidentiality made to the individuals from whom the information has been elicited. Our main presumption has been that the union of data can enhance the quality and diversity of analysis in evaluative, theoretical, or descriptive social research. Schematic models, devised to illustrate the process of merging records, have been useful in demonstrating that the strategies are quite flexible and generalizable to a variety of research environments. The models also assist in understanding how the strategies can be subverted and in increasing the strategies' resistance to corruption.

Certain important features of the process of maintaining confidentiality have, however, been understated in this report. These are coarsely divisible into technical and contextual problems. At the core of technical problems is the need for encoding alpha-numeric information in each one of the models considered here. Techniques for cryptographic encoding are likely to be unfamiliar to most social scientists, computer scientists, or managers of data files. Moreover, there appear to be no standardized criteria for appraising the adequacy, efficiency, and costs of the techniques currently employed by commercial and military organizations. Given the paucity, or at least inaccessibility, of such information, researchers such as Carroll and McClelland[27] and Juncosa and Turn[28] have initiated important research to develop and evaluate methods of encoding information; we may anticipate that these and similar efforts will be useful in assuring the security of information transmission and exchange in a wide variety of record systems, including those commonly of interest to social researchers. But until such research is well advanced, the social scientist who elects to use the models described above must develop his own encode-decode techniques along the lines of the few published examples of such schemes.

Two sorts of contextual problems warrant attention in the effort to form links among archival and other record systems: security of identifiable records and the utility of the merged data. Because the topic of security has been explored in considerable detail by others, I have not treated it in this chapter. Work by Westin,[29] Wheeler,[30] and Nejelski and Lerman,[31] for example, exemplify efforts to document the nature of archival record systems and to find a reasonable balance of administrative and legal safeguards against improper disclosure of records. Research by Petersen and Turn,[32] Taylor and Feingold,[33] and others illustrates how the risks of disclosure can be systematically explored and minimized in each functional area of computerized record systems. Such work is continuing, and it is likely that it will become important in commercial as well as governmental information storage and transmission.

Regarding utility of unions of data, we can anticipate that, in some cases, it will be possible to predict accurately whether merges of data will be useful for, say, appraising the credibility of models of social systems or in evaluating social programs.[34] In other cases, the benefits of merge may be quite obvious. For example, the researcher who merely assumes that institutional records (or his own files) are sufficiently accurate is likely to be disappointed. We know that administrative records are, sometimes quite unexpectedly, subject to distortion from a variety of sources and that systematic documentation on accuracy is frequently absent.[35] Nevertheless, with conscientious accounting of our experiences in merging data, and with the cooperation of relevant archival agencies, we can start to delimit those areas which appear to be potentially fruitful for the social sciences and for archival agencies. At the very least, strategies such as those suggested here will expand the pool of social data—in nature, in quality, and in magnitude—so that the benefits of data unions can be appraised without compromising the privacy of the individual on whom records are kept.

REFERENCES

1. J. Steinberg and L. Pritzker, "Some Experiences with and Reflections on Data Linkage in the United States," *Bulletin of the International Statistical Institute* 42, Book 2 (1969), 786-805.

2. N.S. DuBois, "A Solution to the Problem of Linking Multivariate

Documents," *Journal of the American Statistical Association* 64 (1969), 163-74.

3. D.T. Campbell, "Administrative Experimentation, Institutional Records, and Nonreactive Measures," in J.C. Stanley, ed., *Improving Experimental Design and Statistical Analysis*, Chicago: Rand-McNally, 1967.

4. U.S. Bureau of the Census, "Policy Governing Access to Census Bureau's Unpublished Data and Special Services," *Data Access Description, Policy and Administrative* Series, PA-1, Washington, D.C.: U.S. Census Bureau, 1968.

5. J. Steinberg and H.C. Cooper, "Social Security Statistical Data, Social Science Research and Confidentiality," *Social Security Bulletin*, (October 1967), 3-15.

6. Russell Sage Foundation, *Guidelines for the Collection, Maintenance and Dissemination of Pupil Records*, Russell Sage Foundation Conference Report, 1970.

7. R.D. Schwartz and S. Orleans, "On Legal Sanctions," *University of Chicago Law Review* 34 (1967), 274-300.

8. W.H. Sewell, "Social and Psychological Factors in Status Attainment," unpublished research proposal, Madison, Wisc.: University of Wisconsin, 1971.

9. M.E. Borus and W.R. Tash, *Measuring the Impact of Manpower Training Programs: A Primer*, Ann Arbor, Mich.: Institute of Labor and Industrial Relations, 1970.

10. A.F. Westin, *Information Technology in a Democracy*, Cambridge: Harvard University Press, 1971.

11. Arthur R. Miller, *The Assault on Privacy*, Ann Arbor, Mich.: The University of Michigan Press, 1971.

12. Committee on Government Operations, The Computer and Invasion of Privacy: Report of the Committee, U.S. House of Representatives, 89th Congress, (2nd Session), Washington, D.C.: U.S. Government Printing Office, 1968.

13. R.F. Boruch, "Maintaining Confidentiality in Educational Research: A Systemic Approach," *American Psychologist* 26 (1971), 413-30.

14. N.S. DuBois.

15. H.E. Petersen and R. Turn, "System Implications of Information Privacy," paper presented at Spring Joint Computer Conference, Atlantic City, April 17-19, 1967 (mimeo report reproduced by Rand Corporation, Santa Monica, Calif.).

16. L.J. Hoffman and W.F. Miller, "How to Obtain a Personal Dossier from a Statistical Data Bank," *Datamation* (May 1970).

17. A.R. Miller.

18. R.A. Bauman, M.H. David, and R.F. Miller, "Working with Complex Data Files: II. The Wisconsin Assets and Income Studies Archive," in R.L. Biscoe, *Data Bases, Computers, and the Social Sciences*, New York: Wiley-Interscience, 1970; Steinberg and Pritzker.

19. M.H. Hansen, "Insuring Confidentiality of Individual Records in Data Storage and Retrieval for Statistical Purposes," paper presented at 1971 Fall Joint Computer Conference (AFIPS), Las Vegas, 1971; R.F. Boruch, "Relations Among the Randomized Response Models and Their Pertinence to Confidential-

ity of Social Data," unpublished manuscript, Psychology Department, Northwestern University, 1972.

20. E.g., H. Thoni, "Transformations of Variables Used in the Analysis of Experimental and Observational Data: A Review," *Statistical Laboratory, Technical Report No. 7*, Ames, Iowa: Iowa State University, 1967.

21. E.L. Feige and H.W. Watts, *Partial Aggregation of Micro-economic Data*, Financial and Fiscal Research Workshop Paper No. 6601, Madison, Wisc.: University of Wisconsin, 1963.

22. Committee on Government Operations; *Valparaiso Law Review*, "Legal Note: Social Research and Privileged Data," *Valparaiso University Law Review* 4 (2), (1970), 368-99.

23. P.H. Rossi, W.E. Groves, and D. Grafstein, "Life Styles and Campus Communities," pamphlet-questionnaire, Baltimore: Johns Hopkins University Department of Social Relations, 1971.

24. R.F. Boruch.

25. E. Manniche and D.P. Hayes, "Respondent Anonymity and Data Matching," *Public Opinion Quarterly* 21 (3), (1957), 384-88.

26. R.F. Boruch.

27. J.M. Carroll and P.M. McClelland, "Fast 'Infinite-key' Transformations for Resource Sharing Systems," Paper #191, London, Ontario: University of Western Ontario, 1970. (Also in *Proceedings of the Fall Joint Computer Conference*, 1970.)

28. M.L. Juncosa and R. Turn, "Research in Protection of Privacy of Personal Information in Data Banks: Theoretical and Technical Aspects," unpublished research proposal, Santa Monica, Calif.: Rand Corporation, 1971.

29. A.F. Westin, *Privacy and Freedom*, New York: Atheneum, 1967; *Information Technology in a Democracy*.

30. S. Wheeler, ed., *Files and Dossiers in American Life*, New York: Russell Sage Foundation, 1969.

31. P. Nejelski and L.M. Lerman, "A Researcher Subject Testimonial Privilege: What To Do Before the Subpoena Arrives," *Wisconsin Law Review* (1971), 1085-1148.

32. Petersen and Turn.

33. R.L. Taylor and R.S. Feingold, "Computer Data Protection," *Industrial Security* (August 1970), 20-29.

34. D.T. Campbell, "Methods for the Experimenting Society," *American Psychologist*, forthcoming.

35. Committee on Government Operations; H. Grubert, "How Much Do Agencies Know About Error Structure?" in *Federal Statistics: Report of the President's Commission*, Vol. II, Washington, D.C.: U.S. Government Printing Office, 1971.

Chapter Seven

Prestige and the Researcher's Accountability

G.O.W. Mueller

"AT THIS POINT IN TIME"

I propose to address the problem of "Research in Conflict with Law and Ethics" from the prospective of only one of the human elements involved: the human element of the researcher himself. What is the right power or leverage at the researcher's disposition in order to gain access to material in the possession of others (government agencies or private individuals) which these others may wish to withhold from researchers for fear that unethical, inhumane, or obnoxious facts, data, or practices may be uncovered, possibly leading to unwanted reform of entrenched practices?

Unless the researcher penetrates the armor of protection, he cannot obtain research data which ultimately may be subpoenaed from him.

This view of the matter necessarily leads to a focus on the status of the researcher within the society he is supposed to serve. Consequently, I propose to analyze the view which line organizations (especially government) take of the researcher. Far from seeing the researcher as an invader of the privacy of individuals, I see him as a protector of the rights of the public vis-à-vis leviathanic government.

The Nixon administration gained recognition for its remarkable success in inventing governmental strategies. One of the most amazing among them was the so-called "protective reaction," practiced in the bombing of North Vietnam, the invasion of Cambodia, and the promulgation of a set of standards or regulations to protect the privacy of the American citizen against unwarranted intrusion by researchers. It is interesting that the president should have chosen the television mass media to address the nation on this topic at a time when his administration was under severe attack for governmental operations that had become totally oblivious to the right of privacy. The "protective reaction," however, found the research community to be the scapegoats.

The proposed guidelines, as it turns out on closer examination, simply would authorize government agencies to withhold government documents and data pertaining to individual criminal records for use in employment or credit investigations, a type of research with which the research community, as such, has nothing to do.[1] While this is an entirely admirable move, it can hardly be viewed as anything but a maneuver to detract from the real issue with which the American government and public—and I suspect those of other nations as well—are confronted in this day and age: the intense desire of government to conceal from the public what it knows, and the equally intense desire of government to gain the private knowledge of its citizens, or at least of some of them. This is an issue of law and of ethics, an issue on which the very survival of democracy depends.

The issue is complicated by the fact that information gatherers and custodians belong to the research community as much as those who would like to utilize and analyze the information so gathered and stored. The members of the research community, far from being the monolithic group of good guys they are frequently made out to be by us good-guy researchers, really are a rag tag of professionals, mad scientists, prodders, and doorbell ringers with totally divergent interests. This total divergence depends not only on the basis of their training but also on their mission and the status of their employment—whether governmental, and if so in which branch, or private, corporate or individual, commercial or scientific, defense or prosecution. It depends particularly on the mission in which the researcher is engaged, i.e., his goal orientation. To make matters worse, few researchers have a harmonious goal assignment, but most have to fulfill conflicting missions, e.g., as "pure researchers," "treaters," "reformers," and "administrators" simultaneously.

Thus, to search for a policy in resolution of these "conflicts between law and ethics" in research may prove to be as futile as Ponce de Leon's search for the fountain of youth—yet it may keep us young as long as we search, and will let us age only when we give up.

THE STIGMATIZATION OF RESEARCHERS: RESEARCHERS
AS A MENACE AND AN EVIL

The Menace

I propose that we search for something that is common to all researchers, so that while the search for the fountain of youth continues we might at least have a common identity. Unfortunately it may turn out that what we have in common derives as much to our doom as the diversity which condemns us to doom ab initio.

Here are my two basic propositions:

1. Researchers are evil people, and
2. Researchers can't win.

These are the stigmati which the rest of the world has bestowed upon us. Stigmati, as Shlomo Shoham taught us in *The Mark of Cain*, are bestowed upon those whom you fear, who are a threat to your order. We have all felt the effects of such fears and imagined threats. As a very young cop, a generation ago, I had the audacity to suggest to my commanding officer that our organization was doing a lot of stupid, routinely asinine jobs, which were neither efficient nor humane. Since none of us in this command knew how to change things, I suggested that I obtain an unpaid leave to go to a university—the seat of all ultimate wisdom—to learn how to do things better. Of course, today I know that one doesn't learn how to do things better at universities, but at that time I thought so. My commanding officer also thought so. He felt threatened and feared that research into our mess might lead to change. Change disturbs equilibrium. He consequently suggested that I take my leave, permanently and forever, without pay. Well, ever since then I have been a researcher or an equilibrium disturber.

When the Chicago jury project in the 1950s researched the jury—a project that had me aboard—an outraged Congress passed 18 U.S.C. § 1508, outlawing the researchers' tampering with the sacred cow of the common law.

Nothing seems more threatening to the guardians of the status quo than an analysis of the facts and the prospect of change. Every major research project in criminal justice that I know of has been initially opposed, often viciously. Some of us have personally and directly felt such opposition—whether in the case of the National Commission on Obscenity and Pornography, in the Prevost Commission work, or in our work for the United Nations on the Implementation of the United Nations Standard Minimum Rules for the Treatment of Prisoners, when the representatives of most noncomplying nations feared nothing more than our uncovering—through research—of the fact of noncompliance. I could multiply these examples, but will restrict myself to one example of particular significance, since it involves as research objects our colleagues in criminal-justice research themselves. We recently completed a three-year empirical project evaluating the working techniques, methods, and impact of the International Association of Penal Law—the world organization of scholars in criminal justice. The vast majority of our scholar-members abroad opposed our research efforts vigorously to the last day. The report and findings, now in print, spell change. That is why the project had been opposed.

The Evil

For the sake of simplicity, I would like to divide the people of the world into two groups, researchers and nonresearchers, realizing full well that both of these groups could be further subdivided, particularly the nonresearchers, into consumers of research, victims of research, commissioners of research, etc. I surmise, however, that all nonresearchers hold certain truths to be self-evident. These include the following:

1. Researchers are undemocratic because they claim to have a specialized knowledge superior to the generalist knowledge of everyone else. Researchers are Socratic—deserving the hemlock. Researchers by their very being violate the sacred American Jacksonian principle that everybody is as good as everybody else.

2. What is worse, researchers are antiestablishmentarian, anti pre-or conservative, since their activities are premised on the belief in the need for change, and, more likely than not, their products spell change and thus disquiet and additional work. (I would like to call this the Agnewstic principle, since Mr. Agnew, before he became a convict and while he was still vice president, always delighted in raking us researchers over the coals for the reasons just mentioned.)

3. Researchers are agnostics or worse because they challenge the existing gods and threaten the charisma of the priests, i.e., government administrators. We may want to call this the Weberian or agnostic principle.

4. Researchers are unfriendly because in the process of research and demonstration, they will hurt everybody's feelings by demonstrating that those researched are likely to have done useless, foolish, or inefficient things.

HOW TO GET RID OF RESEARCHERS AND WHAT IF YOU CAN'T?

If it is true that researchers are felt to be a menace and evil and undemocratic and antiestablishmentarian and agnostic and unfriendly, it would seem to follow that the whole world of nonresearchers would mobilize against them. And, indeed, this is what happens to all of us at least once in our lives, and in some cases more often. Nonresearchers will go to any length to remove the research menace. Here are some typical response patterns:

1. One can legislate researchers or their methods and sources out of existence. This happened to the already-mentioned Chicago jury project when Congress prohibited so-called jury tampering in 18 U.S.C. § 1508.

2. A more common method is the simple withholding of research budgets. This will result not only in a drop in morale, but also in decreased project continuity and thus in decreased project efficiency, to which, in turn, the nonresearchers can point with glee.

3. Occasionally, line organizations will employ the research hatchet man, who is ordinarily a research renegade who might have lost his job under method 2, and is now employed to create disunity in the project or to cast doubt on methods and findings. He is frequently known as the evaluator.

4. Appoint political hacks to research positions, and particularly into the administration of research. The Nixon administration practiced this method widely, which up to this point is unexcelled in creating disrepute for real researchers since, unhappily, political hacks are outwardly indistinguishable from researchers. Features like Lombrosian ear lobes, receding foreheads, prolonged arms, etc. have not yet been identified among political hacks as contrasted with researchers, although I would not be surprised if someday they were to be found.

5. Certain administrators have endeavored to remove the research menace by rendering the research-funding agencies so incompetent that they are incapable of evaluating the applications or doling out and administering the funds or evaluating the results. This method, in the current Republican administration, closely competes with the just-described political hack method.

6. It is always possible to impeach unwanted researchers. When my colleague Norman Redlich joined the Warren Commission, he was charged with being a Communist and living in Eleanor Roosevelt's apartment, and we all know through Egil Krogh's testimony that it was the purpose of the White House Plumber's burglary to find psychiatric reports which might make researcher Ellsberg look like a nut.

7. As a last resort, to remove the research threat, one can always send two research outfits in to do the job. In all probability they will destroy each other or reach hopelessly conflicting results.

The devices for getting rid of researchers are so facile, and there are so many more nonresearchers in the world than researchers, that it would seem to follow inevitably that researchers will soon be stamped out. But that is what it said on the crab-grass-killer package!

The methods for getting rid of researchers have not quite worked. Researchers are, indeed, like crab grass—hard to stamp out and multiplying fast. Amazing though it may seem, we all have witnessed a greater acceptance of researchers in recent years. This does not mean that nonresearchers, and particularly line agencies, have accepted us researchers. It simply means that they had to change their tactics in efforts to remove or control the research menace. Here are some examples of these tactics; most of which derive ample precedent from historical analogy. But it must at once be pointed out that each of these tactics has defects from the point of view of the line agencies, which can be turned to the researcher's advantage.

1. If researchers won't go away, call them fools and let people laugh at them. This is the "court jester" tactic. But it has one flaw—it overlooks the historical fact that in the courts of absolute monarchs, court jesters were the only people enjoying true freedom, and thus power to create change, even in the minds of despots.

2. If researchers won't go away, flirt with them, don't take them seriously but tolerate and enjoy them. I would like to call this the "courtesan" tactic, or the "kept woman" or "Madame Pompador" approach. It has a very similar flaw—Rococo coquettes did, after all, gain a lot of power at court.

3. The "token black" tactic is quite in vogue today. One doesn't really want to integrate one's line agency with research, but one must make a show of it in the front office or behind the glass door next to it where the sign says "Research Department." The trouble is that token blacks keep multiplying and gaining influence—like court jesters and courtesans.

4. The burial-detachment use of researchers is an old method long practiced by Parliament (the royal commissions) and presidents. True, though many social issues have been temporarily buried, some have risen from their graves. But more important, the social issues of our time have been so odious and the efforts to bury them so frequent that those frequent efforts at burying the very same social issues—especially in criminal justice—have created such a penetrating stench that the issues can no longer be overlooked, or rather, oversmelled.

Several lesser methods have been employed to render researchers ineffective if they won't go away, e.g.:

5. The runaround solution: simply keep researchers going in circles.

6. The spinoff amelioration: everybody knows that once an

effective change has been created and demonstrated by the researcher it will surely lose much of its sting when spun off to the 9 to 5
crowd which must run it routinely.

7. The antagonization method: antagonize the hell out of researchers by doing everything the researcher suggests "anyway" and
independent of research findings, or at least make believe you do.

8. Assign them to research the obvious.

9. The Caesarian method: divide et impera—split and reassign then
constantly.

10. The "hope for a miracle" method, of which we have a
marvelous instance at CLEAR Center, when nothing succeeded in
getting rid of us, but ultimately our research efforts were frustrated
by the fact that all those line-agency personnel on whose counts we
had relied were arrested for fraud and embezzlement. That was a true
miracle and led to the complete replication of the project.

THE RESEARCHERS' RESPONSE

Researchers possessing a modicum of intelligence have lately learned
to fight back, or at least to put the recently acquired status of
tolerance to their advantage. They have learned to increase their
status, e.g., by success despite impediments, and by clever manipulation, which made such success possible in the first place. Here are
some examples:

1. The *Schlaraffenland* method. A Germany fairy tale goes that to
reach the promised land of ultimate and absolute happiness—we
would call it the land of ideal research conditions—you have to eat
your way through an horrendous mountain of porridge. I remember
one research project for which we had to do precisely that. We
virtually had to eat and drink our way with a warden into the land of
ideal research conditions—to the point where he accepted us and no
longer regarded us as a threat, and opened the door to his peniten-
tiary.

2. The sugar-coating method. The fear of a published research
report is frequently greater than justified. But there is a magic of
words. One could call a prison condition "not reaching the standard
of UNSMR 53" or one could call it a "shocking disgrace." Each
appellation has its time. The sugar-coated finding does not destroy
the research source, the unsweetened method may.

3. The Hansel-and-Gretel approach. Here the researcher goes along
with the mean old witch, that nasty custodian of what needs to be
researched, and tenant of the gingerbread house, until he has her
right in front of that old stove and then shoves her right into the
fire—to enjoy the gingerbread and research.

There remain three methods of lesser cunning and more boldness which have their time, and their heroes and victors, to attest to.

4. The bold response. Let the chips fall where they may. Perhaps the world will respect you for it, and respect may earn you your standing as an honest researcher. Dr. Marvin Wolfgang has used this method with the National Commission on Obscenity and Pornography.

5. The calculated martyr's response. You know they will get you if you take the honest stand—and Caleb Foote did, for which he deserves the greatest admiration.

6. The educational approach. If you cannot reach those in charge now, train those who will be in charge tomorrow and do your most significant research then, when it will be possible.

The question of access to research data is not so much that of the sacred privacy of the individual as it is that confounded concern of government to protect its sources against the "enemy" and brother— the enemy that is you, the researcher; that is Ellsberg and Marvin Wolfgang and Szabo and G.O.W. Mueller. I have tried to demonstrate the fear we have inspired, and I have tried to document that the question of the researcher's access to data in the hands of governmental or private agencies depends predominantly on the status which the researcher enjoys in the society he is to serve.

When there were no researchers, the researcher status did not exist. The first researchers began with zero status. It may be surmised that the first researchers in any field swiftly reached a high initial status, followed by a swift decline in status grounded on fear and distrust. We are today enjoying an upswing in the researcher's status, coupled with an increased ease of access to research data. It would be too simplistic to correlate status and ease of access to data, nor can power be correlated to ease of access. Indeed, for both power and status the opposite may be true. How, then, can we make sure that our access to data and freedom to research with a view toward implementation of research results will increase in the face of an obvious trend toward monopolization of data in governmental agencies? The problem is compounded by the fact initially eluded to that thanks to the proliferation of researchers, we, the good-guy researchers, are now to be found inside the government as well as outside. How then can we act as guardians of the freedom to research, and of the right to keep private what is worthy of keeping private and to make public what needs to be made public?

I earlier alluded to the Schlaraffenland approach, which we used at CLEAR Center to get into one line agency. The object of that government-funded research project was a prison. We no sooner were past the warden's desk and in when we were confronted with the next difficulty. The prisoners did not cooperate with our interviewers; word was spread that we were FBI agents. It took us some time to find the persons who really ran the prison—certain prisoners, not the warden, who was generally known as "the ghost," since he was seen so rarely by the prisoners. We had to sit down and rap with the prisoner leaders and submit to their cross-examination. We had to level with them before we were accepted. Thereafter, we received full cooperation from all prisoners. It is clear that what would have happened if we had not rapped with them—total frustration of our efforts. And if we had not leveled with them, but had been deceitful instead, in order to gain the temporary advantage of cooperation— catastrophe would have followed, and perhaps permanent loss of status and leverage in all future prison research.

Our problems, however, did not end there. No sooner had we gained the confidence and cooperation of the prisoners than the corrections officers balked. If the prisoners worked with us, we had to be some sort of a radical group, and the long hair and blue jeans of some of our researchers seemed to confirm this surmise. Again, it took considerable effort and patience to convince the correctional officers that any kind of reform that could conceivably come out of our research was bound to benefit the lives of correctional officers. What if we had been deceitful to the officers and declared total solidarity with them? I know of participant-observer researchers who lost their souls and standing among those in whose bailiwick they are supposed to do their research simply because they were deceitful. All they had gained was a temporary advantage of time. The real loser was the research community.

The lesson appears to be that we must build a time factor X into every research project, amounting to a considerable portion of total research time, to be devoted solely to creation of reasonable and honest research conditions by allaying the fears of the human objects of our research.

But what do we do under conditions where such reasonable efforts on our part are fruitless, when the custodians of the data we need have a mental or political block? We certainly cannot conduct therapy sessions or behavior modification programs for those past whose desks we must move in order to get our research under way. Thus, we reach the point at which the standing that we members of the research community may have gained by sheer nobility and honesty is inadequate to get access. Then what do we do?

It is at this point that the Freedom of Information Law (5 U.S.C. 522) can help us. Under the terms of this act, anybody, including researchers, has the right of access to public records unless the government agency concerned can prove that secrecy is necessary. The burden is clearly on the government. Secrecy may rest on any one of nine statutorily listed grounds: (1) national defense or foreign policy, (2) internal personnel rules, (3) exemption by other statutes, (4) trade secrets, (5) inter- or intra-agency memoranda, (6) invasion of personal privacy, (7) investigatory files, (8) financial institutions, and (9) information concerning wills. An analysis prepared by the Library of Congress on the first four years of operation of the Freedom of Information Law revealed that of the thousands of requests for information from government agencies, only 1503 were refused access to public records; and of them, only 40 had come from "researchers," while two-thirds of all requests had come from commercial organizations. The most frequently cited reasons for refusal under statute were "trade secrets," "inter- or intra-agency memoranda," and "invasion of personal privacy."[2] It appears that the Freedom of Information Law—as cumbersome and costly as it may prove to be in gaining access—may well serve as an adequate opening wedge when a more reasonable entry does not work.

I cannot terminate this discussion without mentioning the doctrine of executive privilege resting on both the president's authority as commander-in-chief, and on the doctrine of separation of powers, which the Nixon administration used frequently against efforts at discovery and which could prove a formidable shield against researchers' access; but the doctrine is currently somewhat crumbling, and its future outlines are by no means clear. It is to be hoped, however, that it will always be regarded as an extraordinary constitutional restraint, and that all situations not clearly covered by the constitution will remain subject to the Freedom of Information law.

PRESTIGE AND THE RESEARCHER'S ACCOUNTABILITY

Let us suppose that by pursuing the noble path mapped out in this chapter, and by using the existing statutory and nonstatutory power leverage, the research community has solved the problem of access to data. But what, in fact, guarantees the saintly standing that researchers hopefully will have gained for themselves, and how is such a saintly post to be perpetuated? If researchers are to be the watchdog over governmental operations and their impact on the lives of citizens, who will watch these watchdogs? And, at a time of ever-widening governmental impact, the hand that feeds the watchdog is governmental—and the feed is one billion dollars annually through LEAA alone, which accounts for more than 95 percent of all of the criminal-justice researcher's nourishment.

It won't do under these circumstances to speak of a boycott of governmental agencies, of a refusal to research under their auspices, if they control the feeding tray as well as the leash.

The press has one advantage over us. The press does not need governmental funds to serve as watchdogs. Yet, at the same time, the press is suspect of being more interested—at times—in its profits than in the preservation of the quality of life.

The solution that I would like to propose, in an effort to resolve all conflicts of a research-ethical nature, whether of access or of accountability, of disclosure or dissemination, is the establishment of a system of review panels, available to all research projects that cannot solve these problems with their own leverage and ingenuity. I would like to propose that for each of the major fields of science, e.g., the biomedical, the social welfare, the legal-criminological, etc., a national review panel be established under the umbrella of one or several prestigious national organizations in the field, e.g., the American Medical Association, the American Sociological Association, the American Society of Criminology, etc. Each review panel could hear appeals for assistance or relief coming from or leveled against any research team or individual working in the area under its jurisdiction. It would have the power to negotiate and recommend relief, but it would have no additional statutory or legal powers. Its resolutions and sanctions would rest solely on the national prestige it engenders and enjoys.

To preserve unity of policy, appeals from the decisions of the review panels could then be taken to a national, multidisciplinary group acting under the auspices of a prestigious national multidisciplinary organization such as the American Academy for the Advancement of Science or the American Council of Learned Societies, or both.

It may be too early to draft a "code" for the guidance of the decisions of these panels, or of those appealing to them. I rather envisage the establishment of principles along the lines of the workings of arbitration boards. Unquestionably, there already exists a body of "law" that would guide the actions of the panels, including the Constitution and statutes of the United States of America and its constituent states, the Universal Declaration of Human Rights, and other parts of the body of the Law of Nations and the customs of ethical researchers in general. I would hesitate to endorse an effort to codify the rules of sound research for fear that at this effervescent state of development we might ossify that which is purely developmental—including the "right not to be researched." Moreover, codification at this point would stymie experimentation and cut down on the freedom to research and to resolve research-ethics conflicts by imaginative solutions at the local level. Ultimately, of course, my proposed system of review panels cannot replace courts. It is not intended to do that. Its purpose is to add the weight of additional prestige to a human endeavor that already is on the upswing of prestige: research. It is the purpose of my system to shore up what is worth preserving, and to discourage what the research community itself views as undesirable or even unethical. My solution lies in the responsibility and accountability of the community of researchers— and thus on the researcher's stature as an ethical human intervenor in human affairs without whose efforts the quality of life could not be preserved.

NOTES

1. *New York Times*, February 14, 1974. The "code" governs all FBI data and the data of all LEAA sponsored agencies and organizations.

2. See Samuel J. Archibald, "Access to Government Information—The Right Before First Amendment," in *The First Amendment and the News Media*—Final Report of the Annual Chief Justice Earl Warren Conference on Advocacy in the United States, sponsored by the Roscoe Pound-American Trial Lawyers Foundation, 64, Boston, 1973.

Chapter Eight

The Legal Protection of
Social Research: Criteria
for Definition*

Eliot Friedson

During the past ten years in the United States, social research, like journalism, has had to cope with a series of restraints and threats from agents of the state. The symbolic case for the status of journalism was that of Caldwell, who refused to appear before a grand jury in San Francisco and whose position was not sustained by the Supreme Court. The symbolic case for the status of the researcher was that of Popkin, who was jailed in Boston when he refused to reveal the identity of persons he interviewed in the course of his research on Vietnam.

Even before the Supreme Court decision on Branzburg (which included the cases of Caldwell and Pappas), various states had enacted legislation designed to grant journalists testimonial privilege of one sort or another. And a number of bills granting privilege to reporters are under consideration by Congress: there is a chance that some form of federal legal protection may be granted reporters in the future.

The case of the researcher, however, is rather different.[1] First, no politically powerful group like newspaper publishers is available to lobby in Washington or in state capitols for the protection of researchers. Second, and more important for my present purposes, the researcher is a considerably more ambiguous and shadowy figure in both the legislative and public eye. While, as in New York State, a

*Thanks for helpful comments on an earlier draft are due to Howard S. Becker, Carolyn Etheridge, Paul Nejelski, Caroline Persell, Sidney G. Roth and Samuel Wallace.

shield law could define the journalist as an employee of a periodical publication, it is considerably more difficult to define the researcher, who has few continuing ties with any sort of press, periodical or otherwise. And if we assume that social research should have as protected a status under the law as journalism, the practical task of gaining it requires not only political influence, but also the creation of a viable legal definition of what social research is, and who is the social researcher.

In this chapter I shall try to suggest some of the dimensions that may be able to aid the process of creating a legally useful definition of social research and the social researcher. After a brief discussion of the occupational and institutional development of social research, I shall point out important differences between documentary and empirical research. Focusing on the latter, I shall discuss various methods of collecting data and their comparative ability to protect the identity of their subjects. Then I shall distinguish between two distinct strategies of using those empirical research methods. And finally, on the basis of my distinctions, I shall discuss a definition of the social researcher, indicating both its rationale and its limitations.

INSTITUTIONAL AND INDEPENDENT RESEARCH

In the broadest sense of the term, social research may be said to be the systematic and disciplined collection, analysis, and reporting of information about the behavior and talk of human beings. In that very broad sense of the term, social research is a very old human enterprise, as old, perhaps, as the first written, secular histories.

As a special enterprise, it can be most easily, though by no means exhaustively, identified as the work of a particular group of people in society, people who have special occupational roles and identities as "scholars," "philosophers," "scientists," "researchers," and the like. Such roles have existed for millenia, but they developed coherence and stability in Europe when the growth of universities provided them with a concrete institutional framework for their development and maintenance. The enormous burst of creative energy in European universities in the nineteenth century established history, economics, and psychology as specialized occupational roles, with political science, anthropology, and sociology following.

By now, in the second half of the twentieth century, much of what I have broadly defined as social research can be identified as the work of persons trained in particular academic fields and working full time in a limited number of occupational roles both inside and outside universities. As an institution, social research has grown enormously since World War II and is performed by an unprecedented number of specialized occupations in a wide variety of contexts, using a wide variety of methods.

One important problem posed to the legal position of social research lies in the different contexts in which it is performed and the different purposes it can serve according to the political and legal philosophy one subscribes to. Two major options can be identified. On the one hand, we can conceive of social research as being deliberately organized, formulated, carried out, and reported in the self-conscious service of the needs and interests of the established practical institutions of society. The right to perform the research, and the right to its findings, in some sense belong to those institutions, and not necessarily to the public or society at large. In the United States we often call this "service," "institutional," "proprietary," and "in-house" research. It is designed to collect information that will facilitate the attainment of goals set by the institution it serves. Its findings are the property of the institution, and may not be distributed outside that institution should its officials decide that public reporting would be contrary to their interests. It is both limited and protected by the institution it serves. I shall call it "institutional" research.

Conceding that no social research can be completely independent of the established institutions of a society, or completely value-free, there is nonetheless an important practical matter involved in recognizing that there are various degrees of independence possible from the established dominant institutions of a society. To those who are philosophically suspicious of established institutions, believing that they have inherent tendencies to be self-serving to the detriment of the public good, there is a need for social research that is, insofar as possible, independent of them. Such research, organized, carried out, analyzed, and reported by people who are in some sense outside of the establishment and who have license to criticize it, is essential for informing the public and generating political forces that can counterbalance the self-protectiveness of established governing institutions and facilitate reform of laws and practices. The First Amendment of the United States Constitution is an expression of the philosophical suspicion of an unchecked establishment, written at a time when the press was the major medium for independent criticism in newspapers, pamphlets, books, and the like. Most sympathetic writers would agree that the social researcher, even though not a reporter or journalist with an explicit relationship to the press, nonetheless may claim legal protection on the same basis as the newsman—the value to the public good of producing and circulating information generated independently of the established institutions. The problem is to create a legally viable definition of social research that includes independent persons and activities. But what is social research?

DOCUMENTARY AND EMPIRICAL SOCIAL RESEARCH

One can begin to delineate social research by distinguishing two major types on the basis of their sources of information. Most research uses information already collected or produced by others. Most historical research is of this character by necessity, since it most often deals with times so far past that only documents are available. In a different way, most economic research is also of this character, using data produced by the administrations of industrial, financial, and governmental institutions. Like scholarship in general, the quality of both is established more by the way in which already available, frequently public information is analyzed than by the unique and original character of the information itself. I shall call this *documentary research.*

All conventional social disciplines contain within them to a greater or lesser degree the traditions of scholarship or documentary research. In such social research there is rarely, if ever, any justification for failing to cite the documents or books that are used to establish a conclusion or fact. To be persuasive, the report requires very precise citation of sources, so that the reliability or validity of interpretations and conclusions can be assessed by the critical reader. Indeed, a documentary researcher, or scholar, who does *not* cite his published or archival sources is by the nature of the case suspect. There is, however, a problem of documents themselves being privileged and inaccessible to the researcher. In using publicly available materials, no issue of freedom of research is involved. But perhaps the main problem in documentary research lies in gaining access to materials that are withheld for one reason or another by the agents or agencies possessing them. In some cases involving living persons or surviving lineages, documents and collections may be withheld from scholars on grounds of private ownership, and of protecting the privacy (or reputation) of an individual or his survivors. In other cases, governmental agencies which cannot claim private ownership claim instead the right to restrict public access to documents on grounds of state interests.[2]

None of these problems of access to documents may seem to have any direct relevance to the issue of protecting research, but if we recall the litigation in the United States which attempted to prevent the publication of the Pentagon Papers, a book on the C.I.A. by Marchetti, and a host of others over the past decade, we shall see that they have great relevance to the issue of whether some kinds of independent research are even possible in politically sensitive areas when established institutions have the right to withhold access to documentary sources of information.

In contrast to documentary research, or scholarship, there is *empirical research*, which relies primarily upon verbally conveyed information from individual respondents and firsthand observation of others by the researcher. Laboratory experiments in psychology and survey, interview and field studies in psychology, sociology, political science, and anthropology all require access to a variety of individuals who are themselves the sources of data. Gaining access to those individuals usually requires the establishment of some relationship of trust, whether the trust is based on considering the researcher a friend, a fellow-member of a group, or someone who is doing research. As such, most researchers would agree on a basic ethical commitment which specifies that when they report their data, they have an obligation to protect the identities of those they have studied.[3] Typically, therefore, entirely unlike documentary research, in empirical social research the sources of data are rarely identified, and validity and reliability tend to be established by describing the methods used to select research subjects, to collect data and to analyze it rather than by reference to the sources themselves.

Clearly, documentary social research and empirical social research are quite different in important ways. The basic problem of the former is access to documents, while that of the latter is access to individual respondents or subjects. In the former case, where there are legal problems they revolve around the privilege of persons or institutions controlling access to documents. In the latter case they revolve around the privilege of researchers to withhold the identity of the individuals studied. In the Popkin case, both issues were involved. In the hope of gaining information on those responsible for the public distribution of the Pentagon Papers, a grand jury asked Popkin to provide the names of those he interviewed in the course of his research. When he refused to identify his sources, he was jailed for contempt.

THE DIFFERENTIAL VULNERABILITY OF EMPIRICAL RESEARCH METHODS

As the Popkin case indicated, there is at present in the United States no assured legal protection of empirical social researchers who wish to preserve the privacy and avoid violating the trust of those who participate in their studies by refusing to identify them.[4] Without legal privilege it is up to researchers themselves to protect identities. However, the difficulty of protecting the identity of research subjects varies from one method of research to another. Examining such variation can help us focus on the specific issues that must be taken into account in creating legal protection and, if legal protection is impossible, to attempt to make extra efforts to protect the most vulnerable areas of research.

Not all methods of research are equally vulnerable to court-ordered violation of confidentiality. Some are amenable to mechanical and thus comparatively simple forms of control of identity which can eliminate the problem entirely should the researcher wish to take the trouble to do so. The survey, or "public opinion poll" method, for example, collects uniform and therefore quantifiable data from a large number of people, all the data analyzed in the aggregate. In the case of any single survey, it is possible to completely avoid recording the identity of respondents, and so assure confidentiality. Where identity is not recorded, legal pressure to produce identity is impossible. Indeed, in the case of the survey method, or any other method that collects uniform data from an aggregate of individuals, there is no problem of confidentiality at all unless the researcher records identity out of compulsive habit, or the wishful idea that at some time in the unplanned-for future he may follow up the same individuals. After names are checked to make sure that all returns are in, or after all interviews carried out, the record of identities can be destroyed.

It is only when a survey has definitely planned to follow the same individuals over time in what is called a longitudinal design that it is absolutely necessary to preserve the identity of the respondents. These are the least common surveys, but they also tend to be the most interesting and often provide the most important data. The longitudinal design was used in the New Jersey Negative Income Tax Experiment, which suffered from the attempt of a variety of officials to examine its data.[5] The American Council of Education sponsored a longitudinal study of college students and had to develop an elaborate device for protecting the identity of its research subjects whereby identifying material was stored outside of the United States. No matter what the protective device, however, whenever identifying materials exist for such studies, they are not beyond the reach of legal demands for access to them.

However, the survey method is very difficult to use for studying in depth most of the public issues that are highly controversial. It is virtually impossible, for example, to use the survey method to get information from deviant, sometimes criminal individuals who support causes or act in ways that are unpopular or that border on or in fact constitute crime. While it is quite easy to do a survey of public opinion about one sort of crime or another, it is not so easy to do surveys of the offenders themselves. One can, of course, survey those who have been apprehended and conveniently incarcerated, but one could hardly use conventional survey sampling methods to find as yet unapprehended offenders and get them to answer questions. And it is information about the deviance that goes on in the everyday world that is critical for adequate public knowledge and evaluation of the laws and policies of a given time, and their consequences. Such information, collected, analyzed, and reported *independently* of law-enforcement agencies, is precisely the information that is critical to informed public debate and to intelligent reform of previously acceptable laws or policies, and to counterbalance the self-protective tendencies of established governmental institutions.

In addition, it is probably impossible to use the method of the opinion poll, or sample survey, to study high-placed officials with the intention of getting unofficial inside information about what is going on in their purview, what they know from inside an administration about events and problems of public interest, and what they really think and do about official policies—to do an independent study, in short, of the established institutions themselves. Access to reliable and truly enlightening information from such people requires a research method that involves getting to know them as people and developing a personal relationship to establish an atmosphere of trust. Without trust in the competence, integrity, and discretion of the researcher, it is doubtful that officials or staff of established institutions would cooperate with him.[6] A considerable amount of material exists in the methodological literature on intensive interviewing and participant-observation to indicate the importance of rapport for gaining access to informants within official, established organizations, or on the border of the respectable, or in the underworld.

The point of this discussion of a research method involving personal relationships and rapport between investigator and research subject is not pedagogic. Only by describing that method (in contrast to the survey method) can one comprehend the character of the problem of protecting the privacy of the research subject. And in the case of field methods, the problem is that there is no way the researcher himself can avoid knowing the identity of his subjects. The researcher who uses this method of gaining rapport and trust to get at information that cannot be obtained by ordinary survey methods can indeed avoid keeping any written record of the identities of the individuals who provide him with information, but by the very nature of his method he cannot avoid knowing their identities himself. When required to testify in court, he cannot deny memory of at least some of the identities of those he studied. The method itself is such that identity is impossible to protect by anything short of testimonial privilege.

If the researcher is forced to reveal the identity of his informants, he is unlikely to gain access to them or to people like them in the future. Thus, as well as discouraging researchers from even undertaking the study of sensitive issues in order to avoid legal problems, the legally enforced violation of confidence is also likely to discourage dissident or deviant segments of society from providing information to those few who are still dedicated enough to try to study them despite the legal risks. In such a circumstance, the only information available to the public about such segments would be that provided by official agencies, law-enforcement or otherwise, and that provided by the deviant segments themselves, on their own propaganda or public-relations terms. Independent information becomes impossible by ordinary strategies.

OPEN AND CONCEALED RESEARCH STRATEGIES

All the research methods I have discussed have been treated as if they all used only one of what are in fact two possible strategies for gaining access to informants—namely, the use of a concrete social role that relies for its access to information on the research subject's agreement to be studied. The researcher announces that he is doing research, and in that capacity relies in the unwillingness of individuals to provide him with the data he wishes. The research subject agrees to cooperate with the study and does so both on the basis of explanation of what will be asked of him during the course of the study, and his trust in the assurance that he will not be harmed—physically, psychologically, socially, or legally—by the study and its publication. In documentary research, the scholar asks for permission to examine records. It is an approach based on open identification of the researcher and his research, an *open research strategy*. Where there is legal attack on the possibility of confidentiality, in empirical studies, and access to documents in scholarly studies, that approach becomes difficult if not impossible.

From this it may be thought that research on sensitive, controversial issues, on people in sensitive positions, and on sensitive documents in both established and marginal institutions may become difficult, if not impossible, but this is not the case. It is only research involving the use of the concrete social role of the researcher that becomes difficult, if not impossible. There is quite another data-gathering strategy which does not rely on the cooperation of those who provide the information. It is based on deception. It has been used to gain access to information by researchers using both documentary and empirical methods. In the case of empirical research, a large number of social psychological experiments are carried out on deliberately deceptive grounds, some using deception in describing the nature of the experiment to the subjects, others using deception by concealing the research roles of "planted" confederates who serve as *agents provocateurs* among the subjects, and still others concealing the fact that research is going on at all.

At its most extreme, this concealed research strategy eliminates all reliance on gaining informed consent. The very fact that someone is doing research is concealed. As I have noted, this occurs in some experimental work in social psychology. Perhaps because of its highly structured character, the survey method is difficult to conceal, and aside from having it carried out as an unlabeled part of an administratively required intake process for those entering some institution as employees, clients, students, inmates, or whatever, the survey method does not provide us with many examples of this strategy. The most significant method for the use of this strategy, however, is the field method, if only because it is the most naturalistic.

Terminology varies, but in discussing field methods in which researchers obtain firsthand, intensive, usually qualitative information about others, the distinction is made between the strategy of being an *announced* researcher, who asks for permission to observe others and ask them questions, and the strategy of being a *concealed* researcher, who pretends to be one of those he is studying and gains access to information solely on the grounds of seeming to be a member of the group, which he has deliberately joined for the purpose of studying it. In the former case, the researcher role is agreed to by the subjects; in the latter, they are unaware of anyone playing it. The strategy (and the limitations it imposes on the kind of information it can obtain) is identical with that of police undercover agents and spies, even though the purpose of using it may differ. The same techniques of stealing or photographing documents, of hiding cameras and microphones, wire-taps, and the like may also be employed. The research subjects provide data unwittingly in the course of what appears to them as everyday interaction with the concealed researcher. Insofar as they consciously provide information to him, they do so on the basis of trusting him as one of themselves, not as a person seeking systematic information about them for a concealed purpose of his own which includes reporting that information to others.

The use of this *concealed research strategy* inevitably involves the violation of privacy. Reporting the results of the study inevitably involves the violation of trust, even when the identity of those studied is protected. In contrast, the open research strategy violates privacy and trust only if the identity of the research subjects is revealed. Given the distinction I have made among various empirical research methods, and between the two strategies of employing those methods, it is possible to suggest that when legal threats to the confidentiality of research exist and become widely publicized, it is likely that the *open* research strategy, which relies upon voluntary cooperation, is likely to be extremely difficult to use in studies concerned with politically sensitive issues or vulnerable persons. When researchers run the risk of legal difficulties in studying some issues or persons, it is likely that fewer will undertake to initiate studies in the first place. Of those who do undertake the risks of such research, the difficulty in persuading people that their identities can be protected is likely to lead some to jettison the open research strategy entirely and to adopt instead the concealed research strategy as the only way they can get their data. Thus, legal pressure to violate privacy and trust in open research strategies both discourages research absolutely and encourages the use of a concealed research strategy which by its very nature violates privacy and trust. Suppression generates deception. This could be discouraged if social research could gain protection from legal pressure.

DEFINING THE RESEARCHER AND RESEARCH

There are a number of both practical political and general philosophical problems connected with the legal protection of social research.[7] While their importance and complexity may be neither ignored nor deprecated, I am not in a position to discuss them here. I myself believe that on balance social research provides a number of essential services to society, the most important of which is its service of collecting, analyzing, and reporting information independently of established institutions. It is a service which overlaps with that of the newsman, but which may be seen to be nonetheless distinct in its methods of collecting, analyzing, and reporting data. Furthermore, newsmen themselves increasingly rely for a great deal of their essential "background" information on the work of both institutional and independent researchers. Should independent research on sensitive issues be seriously discouraged, newsmen would be deprived of an essential source of independent information and analysis by which they can better assess government press releases.

Should protective legislation be contemplated, however, we must face the problem of developing a viable legislative definition of the social researcher and of social research which does not at the same time betray its First Amendment rationale. A shield law defining social researchers by their academic degrees or by their connection with established formal institutions would exclude the independent researcher just as would a shield law that defines journalists by their employment by a periodical publication. Thus, if the aim of protection is to maximize the production and circulation of information for the public, formal criteria cannot be used to define the researcher. Rather, emphasis must shift from defining the researcher to defining social research, and protecting anyone who carries it out, whatever his credentials or affiliations.

In attempting to define social research, there are two alternatives. On the one hand, there is the possibility of defining it methodologically, as a set of technical data-gathering procedures. Since few would wish to define research by incorporating into law some handbook of research design and methods of collecting and analyzing data, it makes sense instead to define research by reference to "generally accepted standards," and deal with each case in court as it comes up. The problem inherent in such a definition, however, lies in the manner by which "generally accepted standards" are established in court. It is my guess that the most likely method of establishing "generally accepted standards" in court would be by expert testimony from dignitaries with the most widely accepted formal credentials—that is, representatives of professional associations, research centers, institutions, and organizations. In essence, members of established institutions will be the ones most likely to be used to designate what is and what is not bona fide research, and therefore who is and is not a bona fide researcher. Thus, while emphasis on research procedure avoids requiring credentials from researchers seeking protection, it requires instead credentials from those who serve as arbiters of what is and what is not bona fide research requiring protection. Truly independent and unconventional researchers and forms of research would be in danger of losing protection. (Qualitative research methods, which, as we have seen, are precisely those most needing protection, are also those which would be most likely to be excluded from protection by the use of formal academic criteria of "scientific method.")

In my opinion, the solution to the problem of creating a legally viable definition that avoids creating a credentialed elite and at the same time succeeds in delineating research on defensible grounds lies in singling out characteristics of research activity that are independent of credential or formal methodology. Those characteristics are to be found *in the relationships between the researcher and the research subject.* Two different kinds of relationships can be used to justify testimonial privilege and define social research and the researcher for the purposes of protective legislation. The first is one with precedent in other traditional relationships that have already gained protection, while the second is related.

The first relationship is generic to the use of the open research strategy no matter what the particular method of collecting information—namely, a relationship of trust between researcher and research subject. Those providing information consciously agree to cooperate with the researcher on the basis of their trust in his promise that the information they provide will be analyzed and reported without identifying them as individuals.

It is essential that consent be defined in these broad terms, without being confused with the idea of "informed consent." The problem here is to protect research, not to govern its conduct. Thus, the emphasis is solely on the research subject's agreement to cooperate because of a promise of confidentiality, without reference to any other basis for consent. While I am not indifferent to the difficult issue of "informed consent," it is not relevant to the problem of protecting the identities of research subjects once a study has actually been carried out.

The research data would not have become available in the first place without the promise of confidentiality. The public interest in access to the information so obtained, in sustaining a relationship of trust, and in the protection of privacy may be seen to justify protection of studies made on such a basis no matter who does thestudy and what technical methods he has used. Legally, such a relationship can be established by evidence that the research plan was to use the strategy of open or announced research, that there was provision in the plans for revealing the intent of doing research and promising confidentiality, and that there were provisions for the protection of identity during the conduct of the research and the collection, storage, and analysis of the data. Should there be unresolved questions about the existence of such a relationship, no doubt a variety of other devices can be used to generate reasonable evidence that cooperation was voluntary and based on a promise of confidentiality.

The second relationship is more problematic because it is unilateral and not reciprocal. Essentially, it involves the *intent* of the researcher to protect the identity of his subjects in reporting his research, even when he has used the concealed research strategy, when the research subjects were not aware that they were being studied, had not given their consent, and had not been promised confidentiality. Trust in the researcher *as* a researcher is thus not involved in the relationship and so cannot be used as the focus of protection. However, in bona fide research, as opposed to undercover law-enforcement and security investigation, the aim of public information rather than prosecution justifies the preservation of anonymity. Thus, when the concealed research strategy is used, the intent of a research relationship may be established not solely by evidence of plans to collect information systematically—that is, by a research plan—but also, and most critically, by evidence of a plan for protecting the identity of those being studied, and for avoiding the connection of particular identities with particular bits of information.

Thus, by these criteria, a member of a group suspected of law violation cannot claim privilege on the basis of an assertion that he has all along been a concealed participant-observer. To sustain such a claim requires evidence (1) that there was a prior research plan, design, or proposal; (2) that during the course of contact with such a group there was a continuous process of systematic data-collection in accordance with the plan; and (3) that the research data were recorded and stored in ways designed to conceal the identities of those being studied.

In short, I argue that in the case of the concealed research strategy, research warranting legal protection can be defined by the deliberate efforts made by the researcher to protect the identity of his subjects even though he has not struck a bargain with them based upon such assurance. Neither his credentials nor the conventionality of his research methods need be assessed.

RELATIONAL AND SUBSTANTIVE CRITERIA FOR DEFINITION

I have tried to delineate those characteristics of social research that bear upon evaluating the problem of independent auspices for research, and stressed the value of preserving independence for an informed public. After discussing the somewhat different problems of documentary as compared to empirical research, I went on to delineate the kinds of problems posed to protecting the identity of research subjects by different data-collection methods of empirical social research. I then turned to the different strategies of employing particular research methods—strategies bearing on the researcher's role, on his relationship to those being studied.

Finally, I argued that the legal definition of the researcher and his research is in danger of being too narrow and exclusionary when it is based either on the formal credentials or institutional affiliations of the researcher, or on methodological standards of research. I argued that the role of the researcher, the relationship of trust he establishes with those he studies, and the effort he makes to preserve confidentiality even when he has made no promises to his subjects constituted at once legally viable criteria of a generic characteristic of social research and criteria in comparatively slight danger of neglecting to protect the independent researcher and his research. While the argument may not be sufficiently detailed to allow the formulation of a legally useful model shield law, it is hoped that it encourages consideration of means by which overnarrow substantive criteria for definition may be avoided so that freedom to collect and distribute research information to the public may be maximized.

NOTES

1. For a recent assessment of the position of the social researcher in light of the Branzburg decision, see Paul Nejelski and Kurt Finsterbusch, "The Prosecutor and the Researcher: Present and Prospective Variations in the Supreme Court's *Branzburg* Decision," *Social Problems*, XXI (Summer 1973), 3-21.

2. For a recent review of problems of the availability of "public" documents, see Nathaniel L. Nathanson, "Social Science, Administrative Law, and the Information Act of 1966," *Social Problems* XXI (Summer 1973), 21-37, and Carol Barker and Matthew H. Fox, "Classified Files: The Yellowing Pages, A Report on Scholars' Access to Government Documents," New York: The Twentieth Century Fund, 1972.

3. A persuasive argument for circumstances in which the researcher should in fact identify those he studied, and a review of the issue, is to be found in John F. Galliher, "The Protection of Human Subjects: A Reexamination of the Professional Code of Ethics," *The American Sociologist* VIII (August 1973), 93-100.

4. For a review of present protections, see Paul Nejelski and Lindsey M. Lerman, "A Researcher-Subject Testimonial Privilege: What to do Before the Subpoena Arrives," *Wisconsin Law Review* (1971), 1085-1144.

5. Kershaw and Small, "Data Confidentiality and Privacy: Lessons from the New Jersey Negative Income Tax Experiment," *Public Policy* (Spring 1972), 257-80.

6. There are many ways of gaining information without cooperation, some of which are discussed in Gideon Sjoberg and Paula Jean Miller, "Social Research

on Bureaucracy: Limitations and Opportunities," *Social Problems* XXI (Summer 1973), 129-43. But see the articles by Gary Spencer and Bernard Barber in the same issue, 90-103, 103-112, for indication of the severe barriers to information.

7. For a recent discussion of the issue, and a different view of privilege, see Samuel Hendel and Robert Bard, "Should There be a Researchers' Privilege?" *AAUP Bulletin* (Winter 1973), 398-401.

Chapter Nine

Reflections on the Impact of Executive, Legislative, and a Newsman-Researcher's Privilege on the Functioning of a Democratic Constitution

Jack G. Day

Two events in the United States in the year 1972 stimulated a broad revival of interest in the question of a newsman's right to refuse to reveal the sources of his stories. In June of 1972, the decisions of the Supreme Court of the United States in the Branzburg trilogy[1] came down indicating that the First Amendment to the United States Constitution does not afford a newsman a privilege against appearing before a grand jury to answer questions about the identity of his news sources or information he has received in confidence. At about the same time the series of nation-rocking revelations known under the generic title as "Watergate" began. To the degree that these disclosures were consequences of investigative work by newspaper reporters, or alleged leaks to them, concern for the protection of confidential sources received new impetus.

However, it would be a mistake to confine consideration of the protection problem only to the functioning of the news media and their reporters. This phrase is intended to be broad enough to include television and radio newsmen without implying any necessary limitation on other types of reporting. Obviously, one of the major problems posed by legal protection is a definition of coverage. The reach of the definition is a technical concern not within the ambit of this paper. A study group appointed by the president of the American Bar Association to consider "journalists' shield" law has reported. While the report did not reach drafting particulars, it is an excellent canvass of the problems, issues, and values at stake. The report is coupled with six recommendations addressing legislative principles with respect to coverage, the need for protection, the quality of protection (absolute or limited) procedures, and the desirability of uniformity. Important as the news-gathering function is, it should not overshadow the crucial nature of the question of safeguards for other forms of information gathering and distribution. Obviously, scholarly writing and research, whether academically connected or not, comprise another informational entity whose viability may be compromised by the necessity for revealing sources.

Proceeding on the assumption that open communication is basic to a democratic government, the objective of this paper is to examine the place and function of communication in such a constitution. After that examination, three privileges—executive, legislative, and the newsman-researcher's—will be compared and contrasted for an assay of their effects upon the basic operational principle. Limitations of space enforce brevity.

The Constitution of the United States is taken as a demonstration model of a constitution for a democratic government. Any reference to an "article" or "amendment" will indicate an article or amendment of the Constitution of the United States, unless there is a contrary indication. "Shield" law will be used as shorthand for "newsman-researcher's privilege." For analytic purposes there is an advantage in a document with finite boundaries. However, judicial decision, custom, and practice provide a vast additional "law" of the Constitution. In this latter and limited sense it compares with "unwritten" constitutions such as the British. The Constitution of the United States is a useful model also because it establishes a system of checks and balances operated by institutionalizing a separation of power through a division of function between state and federal governments and between branches of the latter. The flow of information within and between governments and between branches of the federal government illustrates an aspect of the thesis that information exchange is fundamental in any democratic society.

It is relevant to the importance of an information exchange that powers that are separated are not divided for total isolation but for balance, and to prevent overreach by any element of government. The role played by the executive, legislative, and shield privileges in realizing or impeding the checking and balancing function is a matter of fundamental concern.

There are at least five propositions basic to the governing model established in the Constitution of the United States. First, the powers of government are divided into delegated and reserved powers.[a] All authority not specifically delegated to the federal government, nor prohibited to the states is reserved to the states or the people.[b] Second, the exercise of governmental power is divided between three elements—legislative, executive, and judicial—not designed to function in isolation but to interact in a way to check and balance each repository of power.[c] Third, strictures on governmental authority are formalized to provide specific prohibitions against governmental action in violation of individual rights.[d] This makes tyranny by the majority less likely. Fourth, the Constitution is written, difficult to amend and transcendent. These characteristics assist precision, make principle less ephemeral and provide a higher law measure for governmental action. Fifth, the most basic of all assumptions in democratic Constitutional theory is that ordinary citizens with free access to information are capable of adequate political judgments and must possess the means of transmitting these judgments to those who govern. From the fundamental nature of this theoretical assumption one derives the principle that free communication is so basic that any blockage of free exchange of facts, opinions, and ideas threatens both informed citizen participation and the checking and balancing competency of the three branches of government which depend upon the knowledge of each about the other to determine when to check and when to balance.

An analysis in support of the free communication thesis could be very extended. This thesis is not confined to a view of the Constitution of the United States. Indeed, one could argue that it is fundamental to any universal suffrage, democratic constitution, whether designed to include checking and balancing safeguards or

[a]Amendment X: "The powers not delegated to the United States by the Constitution, nor prohibited by it to the States, are reserved to the States respectively, or to the people."

[b]It is important to note that an enumeration of people's rights is not intended to describe limits. Amendment IX is instructive on the point. Amendment IX provides: "The enumeration in the Constitution, of certain rights, shall not be construed to deny or disparage others retained by the people."

[c]The federalistic division of authority also acts to check and balance by dividing power.

[d]P.e., Amendment I provides: "Congress shall make no law respecting an establishment of religion, or prohibiting the free exercise thereof; or abridging the freedom of speech, or of the press; or the right of the people peaceably to assemble, and to petition the Government for a redress of grievances."
The first eight amendments and amendments XIII, XIV, XV, XIX, XXIV, and XXVI all represent inhibitions on governmental power in the interest of individual rights. The First Amendment is of particular relevance to shield legislation. See the discussion under VII below.

not. A few examples from the plain language of the Constitution, and the language as interpreted, will suffice to demonstrate the point.[2]

The source of federal authority for the development of substantive law lies in the legislative article.[e] The responsibility for the application and enforcement of substantive law resides in the president by virtue of the executive article (Article II) and the judicial branch derives its authority from the judicial article (Article III). Other depositions of power lie with the states or with the people (Amendment X).

That this distribution of authority was not intended to insulate the branches of government one from the other is evident from the deliberate interlacing of function required by the Constitution.

Congress passes legislation. The president may veto it, returning the bill to the house of origin with his objections. If he does, the Congress may enact the legislation over his veto, but only by securing a majority of two-thirds in both houses (Article I, Section 7). The president is vouchsafed the power to make treaties, but only with the advice and consent of the Senate (Article II, Section 2. Treaty interaction has diminished through the presidents' utilization of the device of executive agreements, which in practice have achieved international accords without Senate approval). He may nominate and "by and with the Advice and Consent of the Senate, shall appoint Ambassadors, other public Ministers and Consuls, Judges of the Supreme Court and all other officers of the United States, whose Appointments are not herein otherwise provided for, and which shall be established by law." The president is also enjoined by the Constitution to inform the Congress on the state of the Union and to recommend legislation. He is empowered to convene the Congress on extraordinary occasions and in the event of disagreement between the Houses on the time of adjournment, adjourn them (Article II, Sections 2 and 3). Obviously, these processes explicitly direct, and implicitly compel, communication between main elements of govern-

---

[e] Article I includes ten sections. Section 1 provides: "All legislative Powers herein granted shall be vested in a Congress of the United States, which shall consist of a Senate and House of Representatives." Section 8 lists the specific powers of the Congress. Section 9 imposes specific limits on congressional power. Section 10 prohibits certain specified actions by the states, and the remaining six sections for the most part are concerned with the details of member qualification and internal governance of the Congress, except for general rules governing impeachments and directions on the apportionment of representatives and direct taxes among the states. The apportionment requisites were altered by the Fourteenth and Sixteenth Amendments. Other grants of power for the Congress or one of its houses are scattered throughout the constitutional document and its amendments.

ment and are intended to effect offsets of power requiring informational as well as other interaction between units (Article I, Section 3; Article II, Section 4).

In addition to the mandated intercommunication between Congress and the executive and the Senate's joint responsibilities with the latter, the internal communication of the Congress is encouraged and protected by the privilege from arrest and speech and debate clauses (Article I, Section 6).

There is, of course, obvious communication, using that term in its broad sense, presumed between the legislative, law-making body and the judiciary responsible for interpreting and applying constitutional and statutory law. This in turn depends upon initiative by the executive or governmental agencies in instituting litigation or by private parties in the case of private civil-law actions. Additional interaction between the courts, the Congress, and the president are evident in the senatorial-presidential sharing of appointive powers and joint house-senate responsibility for the removal of judges.[f]

Inevitably this system of separate but interfaced and balancing authorities originating in a "higher law" document providing an order of powers, functions, and relationships in somewhat general terms generates the need for an authoritative interpretation to reconcile and direct the activities of the operating units of government.

Certainly the United States could have developed a system of legislative interpretative supremacy, but it did not. Instead, a doctrine of judicial review, beginning at an early point in constitutional history, has grown to the point where a concept of judicial supremacy,[3] understood in the limited sense of power to authoritatively declare the constitutional validity and meaning of legislative enactments and to define relationships between the coordinate branches, is now firmly embedded in the constitutional practice of the United States.[4]

Both civil and criminal court proceedings, to comport with Due Process of Law standards, require open access to information within certain limitations.[5] Constitutionally correct criminal procedure, especially with the gloss added by judicial decision, provides important examples of guaranteed communication. An open milieu for every criminal trial is insured by the enforcement of the rights

[f]The Constitution provides the appointing mechanism, Article II, Section 2, for Judges of the Supreme Court and, under authority posited by the same Article and Section, legislation has provided the means for a shared appointment of judges of courts inferior to the Supreme Court. Impeachment and conviction is the removal process for all civil officers of the United States, Article II, Section 4.

scattered through the Constitution[6] and specified in various of the first eight amendments.[7] Constitutional guarantees of confrontation, cross-examination, compulsory process, the specification of charges, right to trial by jury, and the right to counsel are a few of the obvious devices intended to open the criminal trial. Without these devices and others, a person charged with crime could not hope to operate an effective defense. Even the unanimous jury has implications for assured discussion in the jury room. For unanimity requirements prevent arbitrary disregard for minority opinion.[8]

Another commitment to open government is evident in a phase of the checking and balancing process that is often overlooked because it is not a power to check inherent in any one of the three branches of government but exists outside them, and affects only one directly (the Congress) and the other two (the executive and the judiciary) indirectly.[9]

This commitment is reflected in the provisions of the United States Constitution providing for the direct election of members of the House of Representatives and the Senate (Article I, Section 2 and Section 3 as amended by Amendment XVII). The suffrage is wide and democratic, although the word "democratic" does not appear anywhere in the constitutional document. Amendments such as XV (no abridgment of voting rights for reasons of race, color, or previous condition of servitude) and XIX (no abridgment of the right to vote for reasons of sex), and judicial decision[10] have so socialized suffrage that "democratic" is an appropriate adjective for the electoral process.

These constitutional developments evidence the faith that an informed populace will make political judgments adequate to meet the responsibility for selecting those who are to govern. And this faith is backed by the judgment that it requires open access to information as a minimal condition. The election of legislative and executive officials is itself a communicative device,[g] and provides the ultimate check and balance on them while arguably supporting the power reserved to the people in the Tenth Amendment.[11]

To implement the constitutional faith in popular political judgment it is necessary to provide a climate favorable to free exchange of ideas in order to prepare for and conduct elections and to petition officials after election. Such an environment is an obvious objective

---

[g]The provisions for elections have been supplemented in practice by the development of political apparatus such as open primaries, nominating conventions, and political parties. These institutions are themselves communication media compromised, absent corruption or internal autocracy, only by the problems inherent in arranging an effective response by masses of persons to the problem of democratic selection.

of the First Amendment. In addition to protection for religious freedom, that amendment, and the Fourteenth, safeguard speech, press, assembly, and the right to petition government from official overreach. Neither the federal nor state governments can legally inhibit or compel the utilization of these rights or the cognate rights to listen, to read, to join an assembly, or to petition.[1][2] While the First Amendment gives dissent the status of a right, the necessities of government under a democratic constitution may make it a duty. And the public climate must be favorable to the exercise of that duty by citizens of ordinary courage. Dissent is certain to be limited in an environment only heroes can endure.

From what has been said it is clear that untrammeled access to information is among the most fundamental necessities for democratic government. A test emerges: any legal privilege against disclosure of information must survive or fall on the answer to the question whether it contributes to the freeing or freezing of knowledge necessary to govern.

An examination of three privileges—executive, legislative, and shield—will be made in terms of this standard.

Executive privilege is not mentioned in the United States Constitution. Its existence has to be implied from the nature and demands of executive responsibility. History and practice have given it some substance. However, the scope of the privilege, its time limits, if any, when and how it can be waived, and whether it extends to surrogates of the executive is not explicit.

This amorphous quality lends itself to broadening by executive assertion—a condition that is especially important in the light of the fundamental hypothesis that the constitutional system is designed to allow the primary units of government to check and balance the power in each while maintaining a separation of authority. (A striking example of the check lies in the fact that the presidential veto power is equal to two-thirds of the majority less one in each House of Congress. See Article I, Section 7, requiring two-thirds majority of each House to override a veto.)

The separation obviously is not, and cannot be, a hermitic seal. Clearly it was not intended to be. Otherwise the veto and the overriding of the veto, the placing of money power in the Congress, advice and consent of the Senate as prerequisite to certain executive and judicial appointments and in the ratification of treaties, would not be in the Constitution, to say nothing of implicit interfacing between separated but balancing authorities.

Because the Constitution requires interaction in order to balance, the executive privilege poses an unusually critical impediment to governmental functioning if it is too broadly defined and is unreviewable by any element of government save the executive which asserts the privilege.[13]

A critical aspect of the executive privilege is that it is available to a president only because he holds the office. Thus, it is not a personal privilege but one dependent on status and, arguably, incumbency. And, in the sense that the president is the agent of the whole populace[h] in a way not paralleled by any of the other governmental components, the privilege is one peculiarly liable to negation by popular demand. That there is no mechanism for measuring this demand, nor implementing it, does not impair the logic of the point. The weight of public opinion may supply, by inducing an executive response, what legal and constitutional machinery do not. It is arguable that an investigation looking into the question of impeachment of a president suspends the operation of the privilege because it belongs in a peculiar sense to the office rather than the man. Thus, it may well be that when the people's representatives, i.e., the House of Representatives, investigates impeachment, waiver of executive privilege is not an executive perogative. For abrogation of the privilege at this juncture is logically a minimal condition for the free flow of information necessary to determine whether the executive needs checking.

All of this tells for a narrow executive privilege, or one subject to waiver in well-defined circumstances, both because the privilege is not personal to the president in the usual sense of "personal" and because its exercise may impede a basic governmental function. The latter point is especially relevant, and assumes a particular gravity, when it is the impeachment process *directed at the executive* that the executive privilege blocks.

It seems probable that even in the trial of an impeachment, a chief executive would retain the personal privilege against self-incrimination in any matter in which his personal criminality was an issue. However, it is unlikely that this privilege or Fourth Amendment rights[i] would block access to presidential papers, tapes, or records (at

[h]This is by reason of his whole nation constituency—a situation without constitutional comparison except for the office of vice-president. And the occupant of that office, at worst, is no more than emergency stand-in for the chief executive, unless circumstances arise causing the vice-president to become president. See Amendments XX and XXV on succession to the presidency.

[i]Amendment IV: "The right of the people to be secure in their persons, houses, papers, and effects, against unreasonable searches and seizures, shall not be violated, and no Warrants shall issue, but upon probable cause, supported by Oath or affirmation, and particularly describing the place to be searched, and the persons or things to be seized."

least to those having a public character) when needed for the judicial or impeachment process. Obviously, it will not always be easy to determine when the nature of such materials is public or private.

There have not been many occasions for the Supreme Court of the United States to consider in any particular the internal communications of the Congress. However, the Speech and Debate Clause[j] (together with the privilege from the Arrest Clause it is the principal protection for legislative communication) has been interpreted in an eloquent judicial statement of the rationale for free legislative debate. The philosophy and objective of the clause was spelled out in *Powell v. McCormack:*[14]

> The clause not only provides a defense on the merits but also protects a legislator from the burden of defending himself. . . .
> Our cases make it clear that the legislative immunity created by the Speech or Debate Clause performs an important function in representative government. It insures that legislators are free to represent the interests of their constituents without fear that they will be later called to task in the courts for that representation. Thus, in Tenney v. Brandhove, supra, at 373, 95 L Ed at 1025, the Court quoted the writings of James Wilson as illuminating the reason for legislative immunity: "In order to enable and encourage a representative of the publick to discharge his publick trust with firmness and success, it is indispensably necessary, that he should enjoy the fullest liberty of speech, and that he should be protected from the resentment of every one, however powerful, to whom the exercise of that liberty may occasion offence."[15]

The Powell case embraced the view of the breadth of the privilege expressed in *Kilbourn v. Thompson,*[16] saying:

> It would be a "narrow view" to confine the protection of the Speech or Debate Clause to words spoken in debate. Committee reports, resolutions, and the act of voting are equally covered, as are "things generally done in a session of the House by one of its members in relation to the business before it."[17]

If it is a correct assessment that a democratic constitution requires the free flow of information to function, and the judicial system is part of the constitutional scheme with its own informational requirements, it is evident that legal immunity from the duty to provide

---

[j]Article I, Section 6: "[The senators and representatives] . . .,shall in all cases, except treason, felony and breach of the peace, be privileged from arrest during their attendance at the session of their respective houses, and in going to and returning from the same; and for any speech and debate in either house, they shall not be questioned in any other place."

information under legal process must be the exception rather than the rule.[18] However, the legislative privilege demonstrates that immunity does not always lock up information, or if it does, the recompense is a freeing up at another point or in another aspect in which the resulting freedom is either more desirable or, on balance, yields more information.

In effect, the legislative privilege reflects a judgment by democratic society that the greater gain for it lies in an open legislative process, even at the cost of narrowing the right to compulsory evidence which functions to ensure communication in legal proceedings. At the point of choice, the balance tips toward openness.

The researcher-newsman privilege, like the executive privilege, has no specific constitutional reference, but is claimed to rest on a very important theoretical basis derived from the First Amendment supplemented by the arguable hypothesis that the whole constitutional scheme depends upon open communication as the ineluctable condition for effective democratic government. This generates a heavy case for the privilege because, while it may cut off some sources of information[k] vital to successful criminal prosecutions, it may be indispensable to prevent the drying up of revelations leading to the prosecution of other miscreants,[19] to the correction of abuse of public confidence by governmental officials and/or their associates outside government, and to the supplying of information essential to legislative action—all matters of great public import. Important as law enforcement may be, bringing individuals to book is an exiguous objective compared to the public values centering on the First Amendment. A judicial opinion has effectively summarized the public interest:

> [There is] a paramount public interest in the maintenance of a vigorous, aggressive and independent press capable of participating in robust, unfettered debate over controversial matters, an interest which has always been a principal concern of the First Amendment. . . . Compelled disclosure of confidential sources unquestionably threatens a journalist's ability to secure information that is made available to him only on a confidential basis. . . . The deterrent effect such disclosure is likely to have upon future 'undercover' investigative reporting . . . threatens freedom of the press and the public's need to be informed.[20]

It is apparent that the information problem involved is, at bottom,

---

[k]For example, some empirical data collected by researchers or investigative reporters might lead law officers to indictable and convictable persons if disclosure of sources were forced, but not otherwise.

a contest between the values inherent in the First Amendment and these necessities of judicial procedure which have to be met by compulsory process.

On balance the desirability of effective checks and balances, unimpeded research, the ferreting out of official miscreance, and the development of accurate data for legislative action seems vastly more important in the usual case, and for that matter even more useful to criminal procedure in the long run,[21] than any conceivable benefit from the compulsory revelation of sources. These factors provide desiderata to justify a broad shield for the researcher-newsman. In addition, such yields from the privilege harmonize with and support the informational necessities at the root of a democractic constitution.[22]

The propriety of an immunity grant turns on its impact. The question is whether the larger informational gain is made with or without the immunity. A democratic society's assumptions approach an absolute in their need for full information. This need is the measure. It is not a standard that can be uniform for all times, places, and circumstances.

The relevant considerations compel a pragmatic test for an immunity. It is the effect of the immunity on societal-governmental interests that needs evaluation, and the fact that such an analysis is required demonstrates that informational immunities are not absolutes. However, the symbiotic relationship between a shield for information and the basic necessities of democratic government invests the shield with high immunity value.

Both the legislative and shield immunities contribute to that openness vital to the functioning of democratic government. The executive privilege does just the opposite. While the executive privilege may be necessary to protect functions best performed when clothed with confidentiality or secrecy, such secret functions in a democratic society are likely to be far less usual than open functioning, though secrecy may be attended with prime importance for a limited period of time in matters affecting defense and foreign relations.[23]

A democratic ethic requires support for those processes which promote rather than inhibit the functioning of a democratic constitution. At this point pragmatic and ethical considerations supporting the shield merge. For without the shield the democratic need for information may be so seriously limited that governmental effectiveness is crippled.

NOTES

1. Three cases were decided together and appear at 408 U.S. 665, 33 L. Ed. 2d 626 (1972) under the style *Branzburg v. Hayes.* The other two cases were *In the Matter of Pappas* and *United States v. Caldwell. Branzburg* affirmed the Court of Appeals of Kentucky in its refusal of a newsman's petition in prohibition and mandamus (1) to quash a grand jury summons and (2) against an order requiring him to identify before a grand jury persons he had seen in possession of marijuana and making hashish. In *Pappas*, the Supreme Judicial Court of Massachusetts was upheld in its affirmance of a lower court's refusal to quash a summons directing a newsman to appear before a grand jury where he had previously declined to answer questions about matters occurring inside Black Panther headquarters—a subject on which he had not written. *Caldwell* involved a *New York Times* newsman's effort, together with his employer, to quash a subpoena broadly but simply ordering him to appear before a grand jury. A previous subpoena had asked for notes and taped interviews with Black Panther spokesmen. The second omitted the documentary requirement. The District Court denied his motion to quash but issued a protective order for "confidential associations, sources, or information received, developed or maintained" in his professional capacity. Subsequently, the grand jury's term expired and a new subpoena issued, followed by a new motion to quash, denial and an equivalent protective order. The newsman refused to appear, was ordered to show cause, and upon further refusal to go before the grand jury, was ordered committed. Upon appeal to the Ninth Circuit Court of Appeals the contempt order was reversed upon the grounds that the First Amendment provided a qualified privilege absent a showing of compelling reasons for the testimony and that unless the government showed some special necessity for his attendance, Caldwell was privileged to refuse to attend. The Supreme Court of the United States reversed the Court of Appeals and declined to recognize a First Amendment privilege "to refuse to answer the relevant and material questions."

2. Despite both plain language in some passages and the implication from others, there is not universal agreement that the drafters of the Constitution did their First Amendment work with cognition of the present interpretation of their words and works. See L. Levy, "Freedom of Speech in Early American History: Legacy of Suppression," especially Chapter 1, "Seditious Libel Versus Freedom of Expression," Chapter 2, "The American Colonial Experience," and Chapter 6, "The Emergence of An American Libertarian Theory," New York: Harper & Row, Inc., 1963. However, analysis reveals so much language supporting on its face the idea that free communication is an imperative, especially with exceptions so particularly circumscribed, that intelligent design is a reasonable conclusion. In any event a conflicting history ought not to block the current logic which the language will support. And, if the language were not there, it is arguable that the demands of democratic government would require constitutional amendments or development to supply it. The evaluation of First Amendment theory illustrates a response of theory to democratic necessity, cf. L. Levy, pp. 307-9.

3. *Marbury v. Madison*, 1 Cr. 137, 2 L. Ed. 60 (1803) (Invalidating an act of

Congress); *Fletcher v. Peck*, 6 Cr. 87, 3 L. Ed. 162 (1810) (Invalidating an act of the Georgia Legislature revoking an earlier land grant). See *Martin v. Hunter's Lessee*, 1 Wheat. 304, 4 L. Ed. 97 (1816) (federal law supremacy).

4. The judicial power is not unbridled. The Supreme Court has announced limits on its own power. See *Rescue Army v. Municipal Court of Los Angeles*, 331 U.S. 549, 568-575, 91 L. Ed. 1666, 1677-1682 (1947) (Strict necessity doctrine); *Close v. Greenwood Cemetery*, 107 U.S. 466, 475, 27 L. Ed. 408, 412 (1883) (Presumption of constitutionality); *Foster v. Neilsen*, 2 Pet. 253, 308, 7 L. Ed. 415, 434 (1829) (Political Questions). The legislative branch could impair the judicial power under its constitutional authority to establish inferior courts and declare the appellate jurisdiction of the Supreme Court of the United States, Art. III, Sections 1 and 2.

5. Such limitations are illustrated, for example, by a narrowed discovery when national security is involved (*United States v. Reynolds*, 345 U.S. 1, 6-9, 97 L. Ed. 727, 732-734 [1953]); requiring discovery of a confidential informant's identity only in those cases where a showing is made that fair trial is impossible without it (*Roviaro v. United States*, 353 U.S. 53, 60-61, 1 L. Ed. 2d 639, 645 [1957]); constitutionally appropriate claims of the privilege against self-incrimination (*McCarthy v. Arndstein*, 266 U.S. 34, 40, 69 L. Ed. 158-160 [1924]); and the suppression of (1) illegally seized evidence, or (2) coerced or otherwise illegally acquired confessions. The privilege and suppression categories are examples of circumstances in which the primacy of individual rights overrides considerations of open communication. The same primacy provides special support for the openness commanded by the First Amendment. See *Edwards v. South Carolina*, 372 U.S. 229, 237-238, 9 L. Ed. 2d 697, 703-704 (1963).

6. See, e.g., Article I, Section 9 (no suspension of privilege of habeas corpus absent public safety necessity because of rebellion or invasion) (prohibiting of Bills of Attainder and ex post facto laws); Article III, Section 3 (conditions for proof of treason).

7. Most of the procedural rights warranted against federal invasion are now protected from state encroachment as well under the provenance of the Due Process and Equal Protection clauses of the Fourteenth Amendment as interpreted by the Supreme Court of the United States. See, e.g., *Mapp v. Ohio*, 367 U.S. 643, 6 L. Ed. 2d 1081 (1961) (Fourth Amendment and Exclusionary Rule); *Malloy v. Hogan*, 378 U.S. 1, 12 L. Ed. 2d 653 (1964) (Fifth Amendment—Privilege Against Self-Incrimination). See also footnote 13, p. 00.

8. However, the Supreme Court has said that the Due Process clause does not mandate a unanimous jury in state trials. *Apodaca v. Oregon*, 406 U.S. 404, 32 L. Ed. 2d 184 (1972); *Johnson v. Louisiana*, 406 U.S. 356, 32 L. Ed. 2d 152 (1972).

9. It is not entirely accurate to put the President and the Vice-President in the indirect category. Although elected by an electoral college (Article II, Section I as amended by Amendment XII), technically uninhibited by the popular vote, a vast majority of the electoral college have always followed it once it became the universal method for the selection of electors. [See discussion in *Ray v. Blair*, 343 U.S. 214, 96 L. Ed. 894 (1952).] The judges in

the federal system are chosen by the chief executive with the advice and consent of the Senate and are removable only by the impeachment and trial process (Article II, Section 4). This insulation obviously makes popular input remote and tenuous in the vast majority of cases. That there can be popular input is a reasonable implication from the Senate refusal to confirm two recent appointments to the Supreme Court after considerable outcry. There have been other refusals to confirm influenced, no doubt, by public opinion.

10. See, e.g., *United States v. Classic*, 313 U.S. 299, 85 L. Ed. 1368 (1941) (right to vote for members of Congress has a federal constitutional derivation; the right is secured against both state and individual action; where choice is controlled by a primary the constitution will protect the right of voter to participate in it); *Nixon v. Herndon*, 273 U.S. 536, 71 L. Ed. 759 (1927) (Texas white primary law unconstitutional); *Nixon v. Condon*, 286 U.S. 73, 76 L. Ed. 984 (1932) (Texas statute restricting primary participation to members of State political parties unconstitutional); *Smith v. Allwright*, 321 U.S. 649, 88 L. Ed. 987 (1944) (state political party making selection of candidates is a state agency and may not exclude Negroes); *Rice v. Elmore*, 165 F. 2d 287 (1947) cert. den. 333 U.S. 875 (1948) (political party is not a private club exempt from the prohibitions of the XV Amendment); *Harman v. Forsenius*, 380 U.S. 528, 14 L. Ed. 2d 50 (1965) (Virginia statute requiring payment of poll tax or filing of certificate of residence to qualify to vote violates Amendment XXIV).

11. Amendment X: "The powers not delegated to the United States by the Constitution, nor prohibited to the States, are reserved to the States respectively, or to the people." The nature of the powers "reserved to the people" is undefined, and it is only conjecture that the electoral process will reflect a popular expression of such power, and even if the elected officials perceived a mandate, any action in consequence could not invade a power delegated to the United States, or reserved to the States or provide an authority prohibited to the States. See also Amendment IX, which provides: "The enumeration in the Constitution, of certain rights, shall not be construed to deny or disparage others retained by the people." There is at least a suggestion in *Roe v. Wade*, 410 U.S. 113, 152-153, 35 L. Ed. 2d 147, 176-177 (1973), that a woman's right to privacy, "broad enough to encompass a . . . decision to terminate her pregnancy" may be found in the "Ninth Amendment's reservation of rights to the people." This suggests one definite element in the reservation of power in Amendment X because the rights "retained" in Amendment IX seem an obvious reference to powers "reserved" to the people in Amendment X.

12. The rights enumerated in the First Amendment (see footnote d, p. 00) have been applied to the states by judicial decision under the dispensation of the Fourteenth Amendment. See, for example, *Stromberg v. California*, 283 U.S. 359, 368-369, 75 L. Ed. 1117, 1122-1123 (1931) (free speech); *Grosjean v. American Press Co.*, 297 U.S. 233, 244, 80 L. Ed. 660, 665 (1936) (free press); *De Jonge v. Oregon*, 299 U.S. 353, 364, 81 L. Ed. 278, 283-284 (1937) (right to assemble); *Cantwell v. Connecticut*, 310 U.S. 296, 303-305, 84 L. Ed. 1213, 1218-1219 (1940) (freedom of religion); *Edwards v. South Carolina*, 372 U.S. 229, 235, 9 L. Ed. 2d 697, 702 (1963) (free speech, free press, and freedom to petition for redress of grievances). On the right not to engage in the protected liberties, see *Stato v. Mechanic*, 26 Ohio App. 2d 138, 148 (1971).

13. ". . . the views of the Chief Executive on whether his executive privilege should obtain are properly given the greatest weight and deference, they cannot be conclusive." *Nixon v. Sirica*, 487 F. 2d 700, 716 (D.C. Cir., 1973). See also the discussion of the precedents on the claim of absolute executive privilege in *Sirica* at 708-715 and *United States v. Nixon*, 418 U.S. 683, 703-714, 41 L. Ed. 2d 1039, 1061-1067 (1974).

14. 395 U.S. 486, 502-503, 23 L. Ed. 2d 491, 506 (1969).

15. The source of the Wilson quote in the Powell case is given as *The Works of James Wilson*, 421 (R. McCloskey ed. 1967).

16. 103 U.S. 168, 204, 26 L. Ed. 377, 392 (1881).

17. *Powell v. McCormack supra*, 395 U.S. at 502, 23 L. Ed. 2d at 506. For some purposes a member of the Congress and his aide are one under the Speech and Debate Clause. But that clause does not protect an aide except "insofar as the conduct of the latter would be a protected legislative act if performed by the Member himself." *Gravel v. United States*, 408 U.S. 606, 618, 33 L. Ed. 2d 583, 598 (1972). And a member's own conduct may get beyond the protective pale of "speech and debate" as it applies to necessary ancillary activity. "Senator Gravel's alleged arrangement with Beacon Press to publish the Pentagon Papers was not protected speech or debate within the meaning of Art. I, §6, Cl. 1 of the Constitution." Ibid. at 622, 33 L. Ed. 2d at 601. The Supreme Court adopted the Court of Appeals position that the privilege extends beyond pure speech and debate matters but " 'only when necessary to prevent indirect impairment of such deliberations.' " Ibid. at 625, 33 L. Ed. 2d at 602. Thus, the aide to Senator Gravel could be required to answer "questions relating to his or the Senator's arrangement, if any, with respect to republication or with respect to third party conduct under valid investigation by the grand jury, as long as the questions do not implicate legislative action of the Senator." Ibid. at 628, 33 L. Ed. 2d at 604.

18. The privilege against self-incrimination is an exception that can be rationalized by a concern for individual rights. However, the need for information may be so imperative that the government will grant immunity. The immunity thus vouchsafed must be at least "use" and "derivative use" immunity; it need not be as broad as "transactional" immunity. See *Kastigar v. United States*, 406 U.S. 441, 453, 32 L. Ed. 2d 212, 222 (1972).

19. This suggests a comparable confidentiality to that afforded police informants and a little more. The "little more" refers to the fact that *United States v. Roviaro*, 353 U.S. 53, 60-61, 1 L. Ed. 2d 639, 645 (1957) requires disclosure of confidential informants' identity where fair trial is impossible without it. In many instances, the shield privilege does not reach this problem. Where the life or liberty of a person is brought into question by research or investigation leading to prosecution, a comparable exception would be proper. Such exception could be on the order and operate subject to the conditions suggested in the Branzburg trilogy, i.e., the privilege lifts when the government or the defendant seeking the information demonstrates "sufficient grounds . . . for believing that the reporter possesses information relevant to a crime . . . , that the information the reporter has is unavailable from other sources, and that the need for the information is sufficiently compelling to override the claimed invasion of First Amendment interests occasioned by the disclosure." See *Branzburg v. Hayes*,

154 Social Research in Conflict with Law and Ethics

408 U.S. at 680, 33 L. Ed. 2d 638-639, recapitulating the newsmen's argument. Note that the "lift" proposition could make the "lift" appropriate upon a sufficient showing by either the government or the defense. Comparable exceptions could be worked out for defamation actions.

20. *Baker v. F.&F. Investment*, 470 F. 2d 778, 782 (2d Cir. 1972).

21. But are the media to be an arm of the justice system? Cf. Mr. Justice Powell's concurrence in *Branzburg v. Hayes*, 408 U.S. at 709, 33 L. Ed. 2d at 656: "Certainly, we do not hold, as suggested in Mr. Justice Stewart's dissenting opinion, that state and federal authorities are free to 'annex' the news media as 'an investigative arm of government.' The solicitude repeatedly shown by this Court for First Amendment freedoms should be sufficient assurance against any such effort, even if one seriously believed that the media—properly free and untrammeled in the fullest sense of these terms—were not able to protect themselves."

22. The Branzburg trilogy of cases may not close the door completely to constitutional status for the newsman's privilege. The court's opinion can be read to mean that the deleterious effects of a lack of immunity have not been demonstrated. See, e.g., the statement in the majority opinion, Justice Powell concurring, where it is said:

> The argument that the flow of news will be diminished by compelling reporters to aid the grand jury in a criminal investigation is not irrational, nor are the records before us silent on the matter. But we remain unclear how often and to what extent informers are actually deterred from furnishing information when newsmen are forced to testify before a grand jury. The available data indicate that some newsmen rely a great deal on confidential sources and that some informants are particularly sensitive to the threat of exposure and may be silenced if it is held by this Court that, ordinarily, newsmen must testify pursuant to subpoenas, but the evidence fails to demonstrate that there would be a significant constriction of the flow of news to the public if this Court reaffirms the prior common-law and constitutional rule regarding the testimonial obligations of newsmen. Estimates of the inhibiting effect of such subpoenas on the willingness of informants to make disclosures to newsmen are widely divergent and to a great extent speculative.

> There is little before us indicating that informants whose interest in avoiding exposure is that it may threaten job security, personal safety, or peace of mind, would in fact be in a worse position, or would think they would be, if they risked placing their trust in public officials as well as reporters. *Branzburg v. Hayes*, 408 U.S. at 693-695, 33 L. Ed. 2d at 646-647.

23. Historical evidence makes a considerable case against the Constitution being fashioned to establish any enclave of confidentiality for the executive from which the Congress could be excluded. Early doubts about specific congressional authority to conceal its journal (Article I, Sec. 5[3]) from public scrutiny may raise a question whether there was ever any intention to provide for executive secrecy by implication. See Berger, *Executive Privilege v. Congressional Inquiry*, 12 UCLA L. Rev. 1044, 1064, et seq.

✳ *Chapter Ten*

The Newsman's Privilege and the Researcher's Privilege: Some Comparisons

Vincent Blasi

Beginning with Maryland in 1896, twenty-five states have passed laws granting journalists an absolute or qualified testimonial privilege regarding their relationships with news sources.[1] In recent years, several courts have interpreted the First Amendment to grant a qualified privilege,[2] and although the Supreme Court in 1972 rejected the privilege claims of three newsmen, it did not completely close the door on constitutional protection for source relationships.[3]

Only two of the state "shield laws" bring non-journalistic researchers within the ambit of the testimonial privilege[4] and none of the constitutional decisions has. Yet there has always been some concern in academic circles about the disruptive potential of the subpoena threat. Inevitably, the claim of scholars to be granted a statutory or constitutional privilege protecting their relationships with research subjects has been compared with the claim of newsmen. In this chapter, I propose simply to compare the respective claims of the two groups. I do not intend to argue that either group should or should not be granted a testimonial privilege, although in fact I believe that both groups should enjoy at least a qualified protection for their source relationships. My purpose is merely to explain how a legislature or court which has concluded that journalists deserve a testimonial privilege ought to respond to the claims of non-journalistic researchers.

In contrasting the privilege claims of "newsmen" as a class with the claims of "researchers" as a class, one runs the risk of overgeneralizing to the point where comparisons become meaningless. Nevertheless, no statute or court decision is likely to subdivide these gross categories—imagine a shield law that covered only "investigative reporters"—and so analysis must necessarily proceed at this ambitious level of generality.

A number of valid arguments can be put forth by those who contend that the case for a scholar's privilege is weaker than the case for a newsman's privilege. It is no accident that proponents of a researcher's privilege are hard put to name many instances in which compulsory process has actually issued against researchers, even in the last few years when hundreds of journalists have been served with subpoenas. The main reason for this disparity is, I think, that investigative bodies and litigating parties are more likely to be aware of a newsman's work than they are of a scholar's work, and thus more likely to look to the newsman as a possible source of evidence. This fact is compounded in the case of subpoenas issued by public prosecutors by the fact that newspaper and television stories sometimes embarrass a prosecutor and bring public pressure on him to "do something," even issue an ill-advised subpoena to the agent of his embarrassment. No doubt some scholarly efforts are highly critical of prosecutors, but often such research will be published at a time when the criminal liability of the subjects has expired due to the statute of limitations, when public concern for the particular crime problem has passed its peak, or when the prosecutor's office has already experienced a change of personnel. These are of course generalizations, and there are important exceptions, but it does seem accurate to say that the greater visibility and topicality of news reports make their authors more likely recipients of subpoenas, and in that respect more in need of a privilege.

Moreover, the generally slower pace of scholarly research cuts against the need for a privilege in another respect. My empirical research into the effects of press subpoenas on newsgathering capability[5] leads me to believe that most newsmen can ultimately succeed, if given enough time, in getting their sources to cooperate without legal protection against the subpoena threat. The problem is that most newsmen, even investigative reporters, do not have the time to negotiate at length with their sources, collect recommendations from other sources, or otherwise reduce the anxiety of their sources. Of course, for the key source of a truly important story the reporter will find the time. It is the secondary stories and the secondary, often verification, efforts on the big stories that suffer most from the subpoena threat. Since most timetables for scholarly research are flexible enough to accommodate a good deal of source cajoling, the prospect for researchers of eventually getting the data they seek in the face of a subpoena threat is on the whole greater than for newsmen. This is especially true if, as in many government-sponsored studies, the researcher has a degree of leverage over the source because the research project is sponsored by the source's employer or benefactor, a circumstance virtually never present in the context of news reporting.

One might also contend that a scholar's privilege is more problematical than a newsman's privilege because the nature of scholarly research makes the subpoena threat less of a problem generally, and also makes the infrequent attempts to subpoena scholars more likely to be legitimate from society's point of view. Here, however, generalizations are particularly hazardous, because not all scholarly research is of the same nature. But insofar as the concern is about quantitative studies, researchers will often be able to protect their sources by using anonymous methods of communication or destroying records after tabulations have been made. Admittedly, these expedients will not avail researchers engaged in longitudinal studies, but even this variety of survey research can be protected to some extent by the practice of storing records outside the geographic reach of the feared subpoena power. None of these preventive devices can be said to represent a happy solution to the problem, but it is still significant for purposes of comparison that newsmen who rely on personal contacts do not even have such protective options available.

Of course, many scholars rely on personal contacts with sources. Indeed, one might venture the guess that a high percentage of the researchers working on topics that are likely to engender demands for their testimony will be of this description. But even that scholarly research which most resembles investigative journalism differs from the work of newsmen in a few respects that might be important for purposes of a proposed privilege. For one, reporting that assumes the guise of "scholarship" is often presented to and received by the public as more "authoritative," and perhaps the public through its political and adjudicative bodies should be entitled to scrutinize the integrity and methodological quality of such reporting. Moreover, it is probably accurate to say that scholarly researchers act as "participant-observers" more often than their journalistic brethren. Should this form of involvement embrace criminal activities, the argument for immunity from subpoena seems to me to be seriously weakened.

Finally, the opponent of a scholar's privilege who feels compelled to distinguish the claim of newsmen could simply contend that insofar as a privilege is rooted in the concern for the flow of information to the public, scholars are less important than newsmen because so few people ever read the work of scholarly researchers. This argument might have special appeal to those who value the free flow of information primarily for its role in fostering an informed mass electorate. However, it should be noted that much of the work of scholars *does* reach mass audiences directly by being reported in the news media, and indirectly by shaping the views and investigative priorities of journalists and editorial commentators. Nevertheless, if the notion of quantitative contribution to the knowledge of the whole populace is deemed a relevant variable, newsmen must surely compare favorably with scholars.

At this point a reminder is in order. Even if the scholar's case for a privilege might be weaker in some respects than the newsman's case, the scholar's case is not necessarily unpersuasive in these respects, for the newsman's case might be convincing with room to spare. The distinctions I have discussed are important primarily because they must be dealt with by anyone who contends that a testimonial privilege for non-journalistic researchers follows *a fortiori* from the recognition of such a privilege for newsmen.

Probably the strongest argument in favor of a scholar's privilege as contrasted with a newsman's stems from the fact that investigators and prosecutors armed with the subpoena power need a good press a lot more than they need high marks from the scholarly community. Many of the prosecutors whom I interviewed regarding the newsman's privilege told me that they are very wary of subpoenaing newsmen, both because it can be political suicide for the prosecutor personally and because newsmen who are backed by their publishers (as most are) have such legal and public-relations resources at their disposal that the subpoena dispute itself can be drawn out to the point where it becomes a drain on the prosecutor's time. In contrast, one needn't go back to the McCarthy Era to imagine an investigating committee or a prosecutor who could reap a political gain by subpoenaing a scholar and demanding that he "back up his conclusions."

Researchers might also need a privilege more than newsmen because the researcher's relationship with his sources is generally more fragile than the newsman's. Since many news sources need publicity to forward their own ends, they will take some risks to maintain a relationship with a newsman. Seldom will research subjects have this kind of incentive to cooperate with a scholar.

Another factor that bears significantly on source cooperation is the extent to which the source is experienced in dealing with persons who seek his information; usually, the more experienced source is less likely to be panicked by the subpoena possibility. Although many scholars focus their inquiries on public personalities, and newsmen are increasingly seeking out the "man on the street" or the rank-and-file members of important movements, it seems likely that the typical news source is more experienced in dealing with reporters than is the typical subject of scholarly inquiry experienced in dealing with researchers. This inexperience is especially troublesome for mail questionnaire surveys and other empirical efforts for which the researcher never has face-to-face contact with the source, because then the researcher cannot allay the source's subpoena fears by promising to accept a contempt citation, destroy records, or employ some other protective strategy.

Additional differences suggest the comparative fragility of researcher-source relationships. Academic research, particularly in such areas as sexual behavior and physical and mental health, will more often delve into intimate aspects of the source's life. A subpoena possibility, however remote, may give the source a pretext to back out of an uncomfortable relationship. Moreover, frequently the way newsmen win the confidence of suspicious sources is by publishing fair and discerning articles about them, articles which the sources can read and base a feeling of trust upon. Since most scholarly research is published in one unit, long after the fieldwork is completed, this technique for stabilizing source relationships is seldom available to scholars.

The more systematic nature of much scholarly research also cuts in favor of the claim for a researcher's privilege. One of the major reasons why the volume of press subpoenas has shot up in recent years is that newsmen are now keeping more and better records than previously, due both to technological advances—the cassette tape recorder has revolutionized news reporting—and to a greater emphasis on what might be termed "longitudinal journalism" in the form of progress reports on dissident movements and subcultures. But even with these important recent advances, newsmen lag far behind their scholarly brethren on the score of record-keeping. In this respect scholars are more vulnerable to subpoenas. Moreover, the fact that quantitative studies employ carefully selected samples and controlled variables makes the impact of source withdrawal especially disruptive. Whereas a reporter can often find a comparable source if his first choice shies away, the validity of an entire empirical study can be destroyed if the respondent population is skewed by the incursion of an extrinsic factor like the subpoena threat. And when a particular inquiry *is* aborted, seldom will a news reporter's career be set back seriously, quite unlike a scholar, who may have a large professional

stake in having access to a certain deviant subgroup of the population, say, or in being able to implement an innovative research
design.

Finally, the fact that scholarly research tends to be more carefully
planned and controlled argues in favor of a researcher's privilege in
one important respect not heretofore considered. While the evidentiary privileges which protect the husband-wife, doctor-patient,
clergyman-penitent, and attorney-client relationships are often justified on the ground that a privilege is necessary to induce the parties
to communicate freely, I think these privileges are more explicable as
manifesting a decent respect for the privacy of the parties. Even if
behavior is not really affected by the existence of the privilege, as
seems surely the case with spouses, the privilege is justifiable because
the law simply has no business prying into certain kinds of intimate,
sensitive relationships. If this is indeed a major rationale for a
testimonial privilege in some instances, scholars are probably in a
better position to qualify for protection than are newsmen. Most
journalist-source relationships are informal, even rough-and-tumble.
Rarely are the terms of an interview carefully agreed upon. In fact,
newsmen break confidences with sources a lot more often than most
outsiders think. In short, when a news source talks with a reporter he
is almost invariably assuming a risk that in the crush of deadline and
competitive pressures more will get out than he wants, or that his
information will be reported in a misleading context. In realistic
terms, the source's expectation of privacy cannot compare with that
of the spouse, patient, penitent, or client. In contrast, scholarly
research often is conducted under such carefully stipulated conditions that subjects can plausibly claim a genuine expectation of
privacy. This is particularly true of research into highly intimate
aspects of personal behavior, such as that conducted by Dr. Kinsey
and his associates.[6]

These, in sum, are the major differences I perceive between the
newsman's claim to an evidentiary privilege and the scholar's claim.
In my judgment, the scholar's claim is the stronger. The fact that so
few subpoenas have ever been served on researchers actually cuts
both ways. Recognition of a privilege could have the effect of
reassuring many timorous research subjects without having any
significant quantitative effect on the integrity of the judicial factfinding process. The fact that researchers ordinarily have more time
to try to win the cooperation of fearful sources is neutralized in the
case of quantitative studies by the fact that researchers typically have
little or no personal contact with their sources. Furthermore, the
greater fragility of researcher-source relationships, the greater poten-

tial disruptiveness to the factfinding endeavor if research sources are intimidated, and the more justifiable expectation of privacy among research subjects are all, to me, telling points.

In this chapter I have addressed only the limited question of how the scholar's claim to a privilege compares with that of the newsman. To conclude that the scholar's claim is the stronger is by no means to conclude that either claim is convincing. I do in fact believe that the case for a qualified newsman's privilege is persuasive, but the argument is too complex to be spelled out in the space available. Building upon this belief in the efficacy of a qualified newsman's privilege, I personally favor at least a qualified scholar's privilege, and perhaps even an absolute privilege. But the exact contours of the privilege I would propose must await a detailed comparison of the competing privacy and evidentiary interests, an endeavor that goes well beyond the rather simple analogical inquiry I have attempted here.

NOTES

1. The state shield laws are summarized in Gora, *The Rights Of Reporters* (American Civil Liberties Union Handbook), Avon Books, 1974, pp. 243-50.

2. E.g., Baker v. F & F Investment Co., 470 F.2d 778 (2nd Cir. 1972); Cervantes v. Time, Inc., 464 F.2d 986 (8th Cir. 1972); Democratic National Committee v. McCord, 356 F. Supp. 1394 (D.D.C. 1973); State v. St. Peter, 315 A. 2d 254 (Vt. Sup. Ct. 1974); Brown v. Commonwealth, 204 S.E. 2d 429 (Sup. Ct. Va. 1974).

3. Branzburg v. Hayes, 408 U.S. 665 (1972). The pivotal opinion in the 5 to 4 decision was written by Mr. Justice Powell. He rejected the privilege claims in the cases before him but he cautioned that "courts will be available to newsmen under circumstances where legitimate First Amendment interests require protection."

4. The Delaware statute explicitly covers a "scholar," Del. Code, Title 10, Ch. 43 (1973); the Oregon shield law, Ore. Rev. Stat., Ch. 44, protects the source of any person "engaged in any medium of communication to the public," a phrase defined by the statute to include "books."

5. See Blasi, "The Newsman's Privilege: An Empirical Study," 70 Mich. L. Rev. 229 (1971).

6. Kinsey, Pomeroy, and Martin, *Sexual Behavior in the Human Male*, Phila., W.B. Saunders & Co., 1948.

✳ *Chapter Eleven*

A Proposed Researcher's Shield Statute: Text and Summary of Commentary

Paul Nejelski and Howard Peyser

THE NEED FOR A STATUTE

An increasing number of behavioral and medical researchers have been confronted with compulsory process, largely by law-enforcement agencies demanding data that researchers have accumulated. Often the information demanded has been given to the researcher under an express or implied promise of confidentiality. The information is often personal and at times incriminating. To comply with the subpoenas would be harmful to the subjects and would discourage researchers from pursuing important and controversial subjects of inquiry.

Interest in protecting against abuses in the collection and dissemination of research data has been highlighted by several recent developments. The similar dilemma of protecting newsmen's confidential sources and information has received wide public recognition and been the subject of frequent litigation. Researchers themselves have for the first time been subpoenaed to reveal their data, resulting in the search for new modes of protection. Increased governmental involvement in research, especially through large-scale patronage or mandatory evaluation of its programs, has led to special problems.

The prospects are slim for judicial protection of researchers, based

Reproduced with permission of the National Academy of Sciences; reprinted from *Protecting Individual Privacy in Evaluation Research*, 1975, which includes the full commentary to the statute.

on the First Amendment, against having to comply with compulsory process. In *Branzburg v. Hayes* the Supreme Court rejected the assertion of a newsman's privilege based on the First Amendment. It is possible, though unlikely, that current state and proposed federal newsman shield laws will protect researchers.

Present federal and state statutes designed to grant researchers a privilege against compulsory process are narrowly drawn, protecting only a small class of researchers. For example, the Federal Comprehensive Drug Abuse Prevention Control Act of 1970 protects only those researchers "engaged in research on the use and effect of drugs."

Prosecutorial guidelines and professional codes of ethics are ineffective in protecting researchers because they are not legally enforceable. While the doctrine of executive privilege or "state and official secrets" has been suggested as a source of protection for researchers, it would only apply to immunize research data collected and stored under the auspices of governmental agencies.

A broadly drawn statute to protect the researchers and research subjects is needed.

THE NEED FOR FEDERAL LEGISLATION

While privilege-conferring statutes have been traditionally legislated by the states, a federal statute would provide optimum protection. Research takes place in an interstate context, and often deals with problems of national magnitude, such as drug abuse, crime control, and foreign affairs.

There is adequate constitutional basis to enact a researcher's-privilege statute that would apply both on federal and state levels. The First Amendment protects the information-gathering process. The authority for Congress to enact legislation that carries out policies embodied in the First Amendment is based on the positive legislative grant in Section Five of the Fourteenth Amendment. The commerce clause is a second constitutional basis for a federal researcher's privilege statute. It would justify protection afforded to researchers who distribute or who have some intention of distributing their information via radio, television, newspapers, journals, or books. A third basis for federal legislation is the necessary and proper clause of the constitution. This would justify protection of any research done under federal auspices or research that carries out some national interest.

The proposed statute would, ideally, apply equally in state and federal proceedings and would preempt all state legislation.

PERSONS COVERED

Perhaps the most difficult task in drafting this statute is defining who is a researcher. In fields such as law, medicine, or psychology in which privileges have been established, it is a relatively easy task to extend coverage to all members of the profession. These professions have strict licensing requirements. There is no general licensing authority for researchers. The solution of licensing researchers on an ad hoc basis used by the Comprehensive Drug Abuse Prevention and Control Act of 1970 is rejected in the statute proposed here.

Instead, the proposed statute attempts to protect persons involved in the research process while not immunizing every citizen from his or her duty to testify in judicial and other proceedings. Two general criteria are provided to determine whether an individual is a researcher.

First, in obtaining his information, the person must employ standards or principles accepted in his field of inquiry. Specific academic methods are not necessary, nor must the individual necessarily be in an established academic field. These factors, along with past publication of research projects, academic degrees, present affiliation with a university or research center, and future intention to publish evidenced by a contract from a publisher, may be relevant in establishing a bona fide involvement in research.

The second criterion is that information obtained by the researcher be gathered for the purpose of serving the general public in some foreseeable way. For example, research done solely for the internal use of a profit-making organization would not be protected by the statute. This requirement is necessary to justify congressional legislation based upon the First Amendment.

MATERIAL COVERED

The proposed statute protects from compulsory process all information gathered in the course of an individual's research endeavor. This includes (1) identity of the research subject, the most common type of information demanded; (2) contents of communications between the researcher and his subjects, often closely related to the subject's identity; (3) the researcher's direct observations of his subjects, a common research method; and (4) the "work product" of the researcher: his notes, memos, unfinished manuscripts, and other records he has compiled, analogous to the attorney's work product.

Unlike other privilege-conferring statutes, the proposed statute does not require that there be an express or implied promise by the researcher to his subject that the information supplied be confidential.

Research subjects generally are sought after by the researcher. They rarely volunteer information, conditioning it upon a promise of confidentiality. The subject's understanding of confidentiality is often not sophisticated. The subject assumes that the information he supplies will not be turned over to the authorities. The *expectation* of the subject that the information he supplies will not be released dictates that the statute operate regardless of whether an express or implied promise of confidentiality is made.

Furthermore, a number of traditional methodologies employed by behavioral scientists (e.g., self-description by the subject, direct observation of the subject, description of the subject by informants, and the use of other secondary data) do not provide the ideal context in which a promise for confidentiality can be made. Research subjects should not be denied protection because the research design or methodology precludes an express or implied promise of confidentiality.

SCOPE OF THE PRIVILEGE

The scope of protection granted by common law or statutory privileges has often been described as either qualified or absolute. An absolute privilege theoretically protects the beneficiaries of the privilege from compelled disclosure of specific types of information under all circumstances; a qualified privilege specifies circumstances under which the beneficiaries are not protected.

The absolute-qualified dichotomy is too rigid a conceptual framework in which to consider the scope of a privilege against compelled disclosure of information. In the first place, whether a privilege is qualified or absolute is often a question of degree rather than kind. For example, a qualified privilege can protect 99 percent of all cases protected by an absolute privilege. On the other hand, it could deny protection in 99 percent of all cases. Second, it is difficult to imagine a privilege that is in reality totally absolute. All privileges are subject to waiver of some type. Also, despite statutory language conferring an absolute privilege, courts may interpret the privilege to be inoperative under certain circumstances.

The proposed statute is designed to provide *maximum* protection to researchers. It is divested only by waiver. The protection extends to researchers who are compelled to testify in all proceedings in which the power of compulsory process is available, including those of grand juries, legislative committees, administrative agencies, and criminal and civil courts.

The proposed statute specifically rejects divesting the privilege in the face of a number of countervailing interests that have been exceptions to various other statutory and common-law privileges. In this statute, the privilege is not divested upon the demand of law-enforcement agencies for research data. While law-enforcement subpoenas have had a significant deterrent effect upon the research process, the value of research data to law-enforcement agencies is minimal. The researcher is afforded protection even though the subpoena is related to national security, crimes already committed, or crimes to be committed in the future.

The proposed statute also protects the researcher from subpoenas by defendants in criminal trials. A court may decide that the privilege couched in the First Amendment is outweighed by the Sixth Amendment right of criminal defendants to compel testimony. Because of this constitutional requirement, narrow subpoena exception for criminal defendants might be included in the statute.

The need for civil litigants to compel researchers to testify cannot be easily generalized. In comparison to criminal adjudication, however, it is rare that a civil litigant will have a constitutional interest in obtaining evidence such as that of the criminal defendant. Newsman-privilege statutes often provide for a specific exception in cases where a newsman defendant relies on an unidentified source as a defense in a libel suit. In the last decade, the Supreme Court has limited the ambit of libel actions through the landmark *New York Times v. Sullivan*, 376 U.S. 254 (1964) and subsequent cases. If the defendant's utterance involves a public figure, the plaintiff must sustain the heavy burden of proving that the defendant's statement was made with "actual malice"—i.e., with knowledge that it was false or with reckless disregard of whether or not it was false.

The proposed statute rejects a libel exception to the researcher privilege in the interest of providing maximum protection. However, the rationale for the privilege is not to protect researchers from the consequences of making falsehoods that damage the reputations of their subjects. Though the likelihood of a researcher being a libel defendant is less than for the newsman, a researcher privilege statute might include a narrow exception to the privilege upon the plaintiff's showing that he has a bona fide claim for defamation.

The researcher's accountability to the research community is also a concern. The research community's interest in verifying, reviewing, and analyzing data and results obtained by their fellow researchers can be met by special procedures, research designs, or extra work. No exception is made in the statute.

WAIVER

The only explicit exception to the proposed researcher's privilege is for waiver. Waiver is the power to divest the privilege by voluntarily disclosing privileged information. Most privilege-conferring statutes confer upon one party the power to waive the protection. In most professional privileges, the confider generally has the power to waive the privilege. For example, it is the patient and not the doctor, and the client and not the attorney, who can waive the doctor-patient and the attorney-client privileges. The newsman's privilege, on the other hand, is generally waivable by the confidant-newsman and not his source.

The proposed statute is unique in requiring *both* the confider-subject and the confidant-researcher to agree before the privilege is waived. The subject's interest in privacy and confidentiality and the researcher's interest in controlling the release of his data are both accommodated.

In cases when the researcher has obtained information from anonymous subjects, provision is made that he alone can waive the privilege. This does not sacrifice the protection of research subjects, for without knowledge of the subject's identity it is difficult for the information to be used to the detriment of the subject by the subpoenaing agency.

PROCEDURES

Unlike other privilege-conferring statutes, the proposed statute's protection can be invoked by any person having knowledge of research data. He need not be a researcher or a research subject.

The burden of proving that the statute applies to an individual rests upon the individual asserting the privilege. Because the statute protects a wide class, it should not be a difficult burden for a bona fide researcher to sustain.

The most important procedural provisions of the proposed statute are the requirements that must be met before a subpoena can be issued. The issuer must sustain a heavy factual burden of need for the information before a subpoena will even be issued to a researcher. This will prevent harassment of researchers by subpoena-issuing agencies, and will enhance the substantive protection granted by the statute.

AN ACT TO PROTECT RESEARCHERS AND THEIR SUBJECTS

Section 1: Purposes
    The purposes of this Act include the following:

(1) To enhance the flow of information to the public.
(2) To allow the researcher to investigate controversial areas with minimum interference.
(3) To allow research subjects to be candid in their responses without fear of having the information used to their detriment.

Section 2: Creation of a Privilege for Researchers

No person shall be compelled pursuant to a subpoena or other legal process issued under the authority of the United States or any State during the course of any judicial, administrative or legislative investigation or adjudicative proceeding to give testimony or to produce any information storing device, object or thing that would

(1) reveal any subject or impair any subject relationship by revealing the identity of the subject or the contents of information received, observed, developed or maintained by a researcher, whether or not any explicit or implicit promise of confidentiality had been made to the subject, in the course of gathering, compiling, storing, analyzing, reviewing, editing, disseminating by any media or publishing any research data, or
(2) reveal the contents of any information received, developed or maintained by a researcher in the course of gathering, compiling, storing, analyzing, composing, reviewing, editing, disseminating by any media or publishing any research data.

Section 3: Waiver

(a) The privilege conferred in Section 2 of this Act is waived only when
   (1) The researcher is compelled to disclose information pursuant to a subpoena or other legal process and both the researcher and subject knowingly and voluntarily consent to a waiver.
      (A) The researcher must sustain the burden of proving the subject's consent either by producing a written statement signed by the subject or his agent or by the subject personally appearing before the body issuing the subpoena or other legal process.
      (B) When the researcher does not have knowledge of the identity of the subject the requirement of subsection 1 (A) of this section need not be met.
   (2) The subject is compelled to disclose information pursuant to a subpoena or other legal process and the subject knowingly and voluntarily consents to a waiver.

(b)   The disclosure of information by a researcher or subject pursuant to this section shall not constitute a waiver for that part of the information not disclosed.

Section 4: Presubpoena Standards

(a)   No subpoena or other legal process to compel the testimony of a researcher or the production of any information-storing device, object or thing shall be issued under the authority of the United States or any state except upon a finding that—
   (1)   there are reasonable grounds to believe that the researcher has information which is (A) not within the privilege set forth in Section 2 of the Act, and (B) material to a particular investigation or controversy within the jurisdiction of the issuing body or person;
   (2)   there is a factual basis for the investigation or for the claim of the party to the controversy to which the researcher's information relates; and
   (3)   the same or equivalent information is not available to the issuing person or body from any source other than a researcher.
(b)   A finding pursuant to subsection (a) of this section shall be made—
   (1)   in the case of a court, grand jury, or any officer empowered to institute or bind over upon criminal charges by a judge of the court;
   (2)   in the case of a legislative body, committee, or subcommittee, by the cognizant body, committee or subcommittee;
   (3)   in the case of an executive department or agency, by the chief officer of the department or agency; and
   (4)   in the case of an independent commission board or agency, by the commission, board or agency.
(c)   A finding pursuant to subsection (a) of this section shall be made on the record after hearing. Adequate notice of the hearing and opportunity to be heard shall be given to the researcher.
(d)   An order of a court issuing or refusing to issue a subpoena or other legal process pursuant to subsection (a) of this section shall be an appealable order and shall be stayed by the court for a reasonable time to permit appellate review.
(e)   A finding pursuant to subsection (a) of this section made by a body, agency, or other entity described in clause (2), (3), or (4) of subsection (b) of this section shall be subject to judicial

review, and the issuance of the subpoena or other legal process shall be stayed by the issuing body, agency, or other entity for a reasonable time to permit judicial review.

Section 5: Definitions

For the purposes of this Act:

(1) The term "researcher" means any individual who is or was at the time of exposure to the information or thing sought by subpoena or other legal process engaged in gathering, compiling, storing, analyzing, reviewing, editing, disseminating through any media or publishing research data.
(2) The term "research data" means any information obtained by employing standards accepted in the field of inquiry and for the purpose of public benefit.
(3) The term "information-storing device" means any paper, recording, film, microfilm, microfiche, tape, card, printout or any other device by which information is stored.
(4) The term "media" means any periodical, journal, book, report, study, thesis, radio or television broadcast, cable television transmission, or other means, published or unpublished, by which research data are reported.
(5) The term "subject" means any individual whose actions or responses are being studied by a researcher.

Appendix

Appendix of Selected
Legal Materials

I. PROSECUTIONAL DISCRETION

A. Federal Guidelines for Issuing Subpoenas to Newsmen: Title 28 Code of Federal Regulations, Section 50.10

Policy with regard to the issuance of subpoenas to, and the interrogation, indictment, or arrest of, members of the news media.

Because freedom of the press can be no broader than the freedom of reporters to investigate and report the news, the prosecutorial power of the government should not be used in such a way that it impairs a reporter's responsibility to cover as broadly as possible controversial public issues. In balancing the concern that the department of Justice has for the work of the news media and the department's obligation to the fair administration of justice, the following guidelines shall be adhered to by all members of the department:

(a) In determining whether to request issuance of a subpoena to the news media, the approach in every case must be to strike the proper balance between the public's interest in the free dissemination of ideas and information and the public's interest in effective law enforcement and the fair administration of justice.

(b) All reasonable attempts should be made to obtain information from nonmedia sources before there is any consideration of subpoenaing a representative of the news media.

(c) Negotiations with the media shall be pursued in all cases in which a subpoena is contemplated. These negotiations should attempt to accommodate the interests of the trial or grand jury with the interests of the media. Where the nature of the investigation permits, the government should make clear what its needs are in a particular case as well as its willingness to respond to particular problems of the media.

(d) If negotiations fail, no Justice Department official shall request, or make arrangements for, a subpoena to any member of the news media without the express authorization of the attorney general.. If a subpoena is obtained without authorization, the department will—as a matter of course—move to quash the subpoena without prejudice to its rights subsequently to request the subpoena upon the proper authorization.

(e) In requesting the attorney general's authorization for a subpoena, the following principles will apply:

(1) There should be reasonable ground based on information obtained from nonmedia sources that a crime has occurred.

(2) There should be reasonable ground to believe that the information sought is essential to a successful investigation—particularly with reference to directly establishing guilt or innocence. The subpoena should not be used to obtain peripheral, nonessential, or speculative information.

(3) The government should have unsuccessfully attempted to obtain the information from alternative nonmedia sources.

(4) The use of subpoenas to members of the news media should, except under exigent circumstances, be limited to the verification of published information and to such surrounding circumstances as relate to the accuracy of the published information.

(5) Even subpoena authorization requests for publicly disclosed information should be treated with care to avoid claims of harassment.

(6) Subpoenas should, wherever possible, be directed at material information regarding a limited subject matter, should cover a reasonably limited period of time, and should avoid requiring production of a large volume of unpublished material. They should give reasonable and timely notice of the demand for documents.

(f) No member of the department shall subject a member of the news media to questioning as to any offense which he is suspected of having committed in the course of, or arising out of, the coverage or investigation of a news story, or while engaged in the performance of his official duties as a member of the news media, without the express authority of the attorney general: *Provided, however,* That where exigent circumstances preclude prior approval, the requirements of paragraph (j) of this section shall be observed.

(g) A member of the department shall secure the express authority of the Attorney General before a warrant for an arrest is sought, and whenever possible before an arrest not requiring a warrant, of a member of the news media for any offense which he is suspected of having committed in the course of, or arising out of, the coverage or investigation of a news story, or while engaged in the performance of his official duties as a member of the news media.

(h) No member of the Department shall present information to a grand jury seeking a bill of indictment, or file an information, against a member of the news media for any offense which he is suspected of having committed in the course of, or arising out of, the coverage or investigation of a news story, or while engaged in the performance of his official duties as a member of the news media, without the express authority of the Attorney General.

(i) In requesting the Attorney General's authorization to question, to arrest, or to seek an arrest warrant for, or to present information to a grand jury seeking a bill of indictment, or to file an information against, a member of the news media for an offense which he is suspected of having committed during the course of, or arising out of, the coverage or investigation of a news story, or committed while engaged in the performance of his official duties as a member of the news media, a member of the Department shall state all facts necessary for determination of the issues by the Attorney General. A copy of the request will be sent to the Director of Public Information.

(j) When an arrest or questioning of a member of the news media is necessary before prior authorization of the Attorney General can be obtained, notification of the arrest or questioning, the circumstances demonstrating that an exception to the requirement of prior authorization existed, and a statement containing the information that would have been given in requesting prior authorization, shall be communicated immediately to the Attorney General and to the Director of Public Information.

(k) Failure to obtain the prior approval of the Attorney General may constitute grounds for an administrative reprimand or other appropriate disciplinary action.

**B. The Attorney General Extends in 1975 the Federal
Guidelines to Cover "Authors" and "All Individuals
Engaged in Reporting on Public Affairs"***

... The news media, as well as scholars and authors of non-fiction
material, have expressed great concern about the effect upon their
work of demands by the government for information given to them
in confidence or the identity of confidential sources. I cannot help
but notice what I think is the paradox of the press's concern for the
confidentiality of the identity of sources in that setting but its lack
of concern for the confidentiality of the identity of the same kind of
sources when the information is given to government investigative
agencies. But this does not change the point that there are important
values to be considered. The Supreme Court has ruled that the First
Amendment is not abridged by requiring reporters to disclose the
identity of their sources to a grand jury when that information is
needed in the course of a good faith grand jury investigation. But this
is a recognition that the issue does involve values close to First
Amendment rights, and the department therefore has a special
responsibility. There is another related aspect to be considered, and
that is the importance of avoiding the appearance that the government by use of subpoenas is trying to harass writers who have
reported on matters embarrassing to the officials of government. For
these reasons, the pertinent Department of Justice regulation requires the authorization of the attorney general for the issuance of
a subpoena to "any member of the news media." It sets forth a series
of guidelines to be considered in requesting such authorization, and
it calls for preliminary negotiations with the person to be subpoenaed to try to work out an arrangement which can avoid conflict
over the issue. In most cases these negotiations have proven successful, so that even when a subpoena is ultimately used, the reporter has
given his consent to testify or to produce material in his possession.
Careful adherence to these procedures is important. In one recent
instance when the subpoena was not authorized, it was quashed. The
Department of Justice has taken the position on several occasions
that the scope of the regulation should be construed broadly to cover
not only employees of recognized publications or broadcast organizations but also to cover all individuals engaged in reporting on public
affairs. I ask your cooperation in this. Whenever the potential issue
of confidentiality of sources arises—whether the subject of the proposed subpoena is a newspaper reporter, documentary film producer,
or author—you should refer the matter to my office for approval.

---

*Excerpt from an address by The Honorable Edward H. Levi, Attorney
General of the United States, before the United States Attorneys/United States
Marshals Conference, November 19, 1975, Tucson, Arizona.

II. JUDICIAL RECOGNITION OF
SPECIAL RESEARCHER STATUS

A. Newspaper Account of *Richards of Rockford, Inc.*
*v. Pacific Gas and Electric Company**

A Federal judge in California has ruled that a Harvard professor need not disclose information obtained confidentially in the course of academic research.

The opinion, issued May 20 by United States District Judge Charles B. Renfrew in San Francisco and received last week at Harvard, is considered to have far-reaching implications in academic circles.

Daniel Steiner, general counsel to Harvard University, said, "as far as we know, this is the first case involving a university scholar where a court has provided protection for research data."

In a telephone interview Monday, Steiner said the case was important because "a fair amount of academic research, especially in the social sciences, involves confidential relations between a researcher and his sources."

University administrators said that forced disclosure of privileged information could cripple the case-study method used by most graduate schools of business. Companies involved in the development of nearly all such cases grant access to researchers only if the companies are allowed to remain anonymous.

In the California case, Marc J. Roberts, professor of political economy in the Harvard School of Public Health, cited the First Amendment—which protects freedom of expression—in refusing to produce his research notes or identify his sources.

Interview Details Sought

The plaintiff was Richards of Rockford Inc., an Illinois-based supplier of environmental equipment, which sought details of Professor Roberts's interviews at Pacific Gas and Electric Company in California.

Judge Renfrew said: "Society has a profound interest in the research of its scholars, work which has the unique potential to facilitate change through knowledge. Compelled disclosure of confidential information would without question severely stifle research

---

*"U.S. Court Shields Data of Scholar: Research Held Confidential in a California Case," New York *Times*, June 13, 1976, p. 29.

into questions of public policy, the very subjects in which the public interest is greatest."

Mr. Steiner said that supporting affidavits from professors at Harvard, Stanford University and the University of California at Berkeley helped win the case.

The statements "expressed the tremendous impact an adverse decision would have on teaching and scholarship in certain areas of the social sciences," Mr. Steiner added.

The judge said he did not have to decide whether academic researchers had a constitutional privilege to protect their sources.

However, he said, First Amendment cases involving news reporters provide useful guidelines for striking a balance between discovery of evidence and nondisclosure.

Effect on Criminal Cases

The ruling, Mr. Steiner said, may not affect criminal cases. He recalled that several years ago an assistant professor of government at Harvard went to jail for two days after he refused to testify before a grand jury looking into release of the Pentagon Papers.

Professor Roberts had interviewed employees of Pacific Gas and Electric in 1974 as part of a research project investigating the manner in which utility companies make environmental decisions. At the time, he made a written pledge of confidentiality to the California utility.

One subject of his research was the power company's plant at Pittsburg, Calif.

Meanwhile, Richards of Rockford Inc. filed a breach-of-contract suit against Pacific Gas seeking final payment for the design, manufacture and delivery of equipment to the power company for use in its plant.

Richards also contended that it may have been defamed during the interviews and tried to recover damages in court.

In short, Judge Renfrew said, if the Richards company wanted information on the decision by Pacific Gas and Electric not to use its equipment, it should ask Pacific Gas, not the Harvard professor.

"What is ultimately at stake here," Mr. Steiner said, "is whether the public interest is best served by the unfettered research effort of academics, and the judge agreed that it is."

B. Full Text of the Court's Opinion in *Rockford*

Plaintiff Richards of Rockford, Inc. ("Richards") brought this diversity action against defendant Pacific Gas and Electric Company ("PG&E"). In the course of discovery, plaintiff moved to compel a third party to testify and to produce documents concerning certain confidential interviews with employees of PG&E. The issues having been briefed and argued, the Court denied the motion from the bench. While this case was subsequently settled on the eve of trial, the Court felt a written discussion of the reasons for its order would be appropriate because of the importance and novelty of the question presented.

I

Richards brought an action for breach of contract, seeking final payment under an agreement for the design, manufacture and delivery of 135 spray cooling modules for use in PG&E's Pittsburg, California power plant. PG&E withheld final payment, because the spray cooling modules allegedly did not perform as guaranteed. Richards maintains that the modules met contract specifications, but that the actual weather conditions to which the modules were subjected varied significantly from the design weather conditions specified by PG&E in making the contract. Richards further contends that the modules were severely damaged because of PG&E's alleged negligence in designing and installing the entire cooling system of which the modules were a part. In addition to its contract action, Richards alleges that PG&E published defamatory statements with the intent to injure Richards' business and reputation, for which Richards seeks compensatory and punitive damages.

In conducting its discovery, plaintiff deposed Professor Marc J. Roberts of the Harvard School of Public Health and the Kennedy School of Public Administration. Under a pledge of confidentiality, Professor Roberts had interviewed employees of PG&E as part of a research project investigating the manner in which utilities make environmental decisions. PG&E was one of six utilities studied. The focus of Professor Roberts' research was the relationship between organizational structure and decision-making. The decision to install the spray cooling canal at the Pittsburg, California power plant was one subject of inquiry. On the advice of counsel, Professor Roberts declined to disclose either the identity of the PG&E employees interviewed or the substance of what they said.

Plaintiff thereafter moved for an order to compel production of documents[1] and to require testimony about the identity of the

---

1. The documents sought were Professor Roberts and Lane McIntosh's notes of the interviews.

PG&E employees interviewed. Plaintiff directed its motion to Lane McIntosh, Professor Roberts' research assistant. This fact does not alter the Court's reasoning process, nor does it raise any special problems of privilege, since the Court's aim is not to create a privilege, but rather to achieve a balance between certain competing interests.[2] Regardless of whether the motion names Professor Roberts or his assistant, the issue remains the same: whether on these facts, plaintiff's interest in satisfying its discovery request outweighs the public interest in maintaining confidential relationships between academic researchers and their sources.

II

The law begins with the presumption that the public is entitled to every person's evidence. *Blackmer v. United States*, 284 U.S. 421 (1932). Rule 27(b)(1) of the Federal Rules of Civil Procedure authorizes discovery of any relevant matter not privileged. Nevertheless the trial judge is invested with broad discretion in supervising the course and scope of discovery. Fed. Rules Civ. Proc., Rules 26 and 37. The exercise of this discretion often requires that the court balance the interests of the private litigant in obtaining the information sought against the costs of providing it. *Apicella v. McNeil Laboratories, Inc.*, 66 F.R.D. 78 (E.D.N.Y. 1975).

The interests at stake here are not easily compared. The private litigant and the public have a strong interest in the fair and efficient resolution of civil disputes in courts of law. On the other hand, society has a profound interest in the research of its scholars, work which has the unique potential to facilitate change through knowledge. Counsel for Lane McIntosh have produced an impressive series of affidavits from scholars throughout the country attesting to the necessity of maintaining confidential relationships if their research is to be accomplished. Much of the raw data on which research is based simply is not made available except upon a pledge of confidentiality. Compelled disclosure of confidential information would without question severely stifle research into questions of public policy, the very subjects in which the public interest is greatest.

The cases most closely analogous to the present facts are those involving the qualified First Amendment privilege of newsmen not to testify. Whether the public interest in protecting confidential relationships between academic researchers and their sources rises to the

---

2. The result reached here is not based upon any privilege; rather it is founded upon the court's supervisory powers over discovery. The Court notes, however, that unless the claimed privilege rises to a constitutional level, the court must look to California law (Federal Rules of Evidence §501) which does not provide for such a privilege.

stature of a constitutional privilege need not be resolved by the instant case. Nevertheless, the cases involving newsmen provide useful guidelines for striking a balance between discovery and nondisclosure: the nature of the proceeding, whether the deponent is a party, whether the information sought is available from other sources, and whether the information sought goes to the heart of the claim. See generally *Baker v. F & F Investment*, 470 F.2d 778 (2 Cir. 1972), *cert. denied*, 411 U.S. 966 (1973).

This is a civil proceeding. Neither Professor Roberts nor Lane McIntosh are parties to the underlying action. The research project for which the interviews were conducted was not initiated with an eye to this litigation. The central subject of this action, the events surrounding the decision to discontinue using the spray cooling system at the Pittsburg power plant, was not a focus of the study.[3] The factual issues which divide the parties may certainly be resolved without resort to statements made by PG&E employees to Professor Roberts. The terms of the written agreement, the relevant weather conditions, and the technical performance of the modules, are readily and independently adducible. Any information Professor Roberts or Lane McIntosh may have as to the identity of those PG&E officials who decided to abandon the system and the reasons for their decision is available to plaintiffs through interrogatories propounded to PG&E. In short, the information sought is largely supplementary.

All of the above considerations weight the balance toward non-disclosure. A more difficult problem is raised by plaintiff's defamation allegations. Counsel for Richards suggests that Richards may have been defamed during the interviews, and that such information goes to the heart of plaintiff's claim and is not available through alternative means. Indeed, there is authority that one who publishes defamatory statements has no First Amendment privilege to refuse to reveal the identity of the source for such statements. *Garland v. Torre*, 259 F.2d 545 (2 Cir. 1958), *cert.denied*, 358 U.S. 910 (1958). In *Garland*, however, the deponent was a party; more importantly, only the identity of the source for the alleged defamation was at issue. It was beyond dispute that allegedly defamatory statements had been published. Here, by contrast, there is absolutely no evidence that Richards was defamed during the interviews with Professor Roberts. No such allegations appear in plaintiff's com-

---

3. Professor Roberts has thus far published one article as a result of the research of which these interviews were a part. It contains no mention of the power plant at Pittsburg, California, nor of the spray cooling modules manufactured by Richards, nor are any of the persons interviewed identified. "An Evolutionary and Institutional View of the Behavior of Public and Private Companies," LXV *The American Economic Review* 415 (May 1975).

plaint, nor, as far as the Court can determine, in any of plaintiff's answers to interrogatories. Given the importance of maintaining confidential channels of communication between academic researchers and their sources, the Court will not compel disclosure absent at least a prima facie showing that Richards was in fact defamed in the course of the interviews conducted by Professor Roberts.

III

The liberal discovery provisions of the Federal Rules of Civil Procedure are an integral part of the overall scheme of litigation in the federal courts. Their scope is unquestionably broad. It is for that very reason that the application of the rules of discovery is subject to the supervisory discretion of the trial judge, whose duty it is to ensure that the quest for discovery does not subsume other important interests. On these facts, the Court finds that the costs of compelling the discovery sought here far outweigh the movant's asserted interest in the information sought. Accordingly, the motion to compel a third party to testify and to produce documents was denied.

Dated: May 20, 1976

Charles B. Renfrew
United States District Judge

III. SOME RELEVANT STATUTES

A. The 1973 Federal Statute Creating a Testimonial Privilege for Law Enforcement Assistance Administration Officers, Employees, Contractors, and Grantees Engaged in Research: Title 42 United States Code Section 3771.[†]

Information available for prescribed purposes—Prohibition against use or revelation of information for other than stated purposes; immunity of copies from legal process; requirement of consent for admission as evidence or for use in judicial or administrative proceedings

(a) Except as provided by Federal law other than this chapter, no officer or employee of the Federal Government, nor any recipient of assistance under the provisions of this chapter* shall use or reveal any research or statistical information furnished under this chapter by any person and identifiable to any specific private person for any purpose other than the purpose for which it was obtained in accordance with this chapter. Copies of such information shall be immune from legal process, and shall not, without the consent of the person furnishing such information, be admitted as evidence or used for any purpose in any action, suit, or other judicial or administrative proceedings.

Criminal history information; disposition and arrest data; procedures for current collection, storage, and dissemination; security and privacy; use for lawful purposes; challenge or correction of information of automated system

(b) All criminal history information collected, stored, or disseminated through support under this chapter shall contain, to the maximum extent feasible, disposition as well as arrest data where arrest data is included therein. The collection, storage, and dissemination of such information shall take place under procedures reasonably designed to insure that all such information is kept current therein; the Administration shall assure that the security and privacy of all information is adequately provided for and that information shall only be used for law enforcement and criminal justice and other lawful purposes. In addition, an individual who believes that criminal history information concerning him contained in an automated system is inaccurate, incomplete, or maintained in violation of this chapter, shall, upon satisfactory verification of his identity, be

---

[†]Pub. L. 90-351, Title I, § 524, as added Pub. L. 93-83, § 2, Aug. 6, 1973, 87 Stat. 215.

*Which establishes the Law Enforcement Assistance Administration [editor].

entitled to review such information and to obtain a copy of it for the purpose of challenge or correction.

Penalties for violations

(c) Any person violating the provisions of this section, or of any rule, regulation, or order issued thereunder, shall be fined not to exceed $10,000, in addition to any other penalty imposed by law.

B. An Example of a State "Freedom of Information Act":
Florida's "Sunshine" Law (Chapter 286, Section .011)

Public meetings and records; public inspection; penalties.

(1) All meetings of any board or commission of any state agency or authority or of any agency or authority of any county, municipal corporation of any political subdivision, except as otherwise provided in the Constitution, at which official acts are to be taken are declared to be public meetings open to the public at all times, and no resolution, rule, regulation, or formal action shall be considered binding except as taken or made at such meeting.

(2) The minutes of a meeting of any such board or commission of any such state agency or authority shall be promptly recorded and such records shall be open to public inspection. The circuit courts of this state shall have jurisdiction to issue injunctions to enforce the purposes of this section upon application by any citizen of this state.

(3) Any person who is a member of a board or commission or of any state agency or authority of any county, municipal corporation or any political subdivision who violates the provisions of this section by attending a meeting not held in accordance with the provisions hereof is guilty of a misdemeanor of the second degree, punishable as provided in s. 775.082 or s. 775.083.

Index

About the Contributors

Dr. Carol M. Barker is the assistant director of the Twentieth Century Fund in New York City. A political scientist (Ph.D. Columbia), Dr. Barker co-authored a report on scholars' access to government documents entitled "Classified Files: The Yellowing Pages" 1972.

Professor Vincent A. Blasi teaches constitutional law and a seminar in freedom of speech at the University of Michigan Law School. He is the author of one of the few empirical studies of subpoenas given to newsmen (70 Mich. L. Rev. 229, 1971). Professor Blasi was the reporter to the Commission on Uniform Laws for the drafting of a model journalist shield statute.

Dr. Robert Boruch, Director of the Division of Methodology and Evaluation Research (Psychology Department) at Northwestern University, has written numerous articles on research methods and data confidentiality. He is co-author of *Social Experimentation: A Method for Planning and Evaluating Social Programs* (1974), and co-editor of *Experimental Testing of Public Policy*. Dr. Boruch is a member of panels on confidentiality of the National Academy of Sciences and the American Psychological Association.

Judge Jack G. Day (LLB. and M.A. Ohio State University) has been a judge of the Ohio Appellate District Court since 1968. He was chairman of the Criminal Justice Section of the American Bar Association during 1973-74. A former professor of political science and lecturer in the law school at Case-Western Reserve University, Judge Day has written extensively on criminal and labor law.

Professor Eliot Freidson teaches sociology at New York University. Professor Freidson received his Ph.D. in sociology from the University of Chicago and has written a number of books on medicine and on the professions. He has been active in the American Civil Liberties Union and the American Sociological Association in studying and suggesting remedies for the problems of confidential social science research.

Dr. Robert J. Levine (M.D., George Washington) is a Professor of Medicine and Lecturer in Pharmacology at Yale University in New Haven, Connecticut. He is editor of the Journal *Clinical Research.* Dr. Levine is also chairman of the Yale Medical School Human Investigation Committee, which reviews clinical research done at the University for the purpose of protecting the rights of subjects. He has written articles on the ethics of human experimentation, as well as guidelines for negotiating informed consent with prospective human subjects of experimentation. Since December 1974, he has been a consultant to the National Commission for the Protection of Human Subjects of Biomedical and Behavioral Research.

At the time of the Bielefeld Conference, **Gerhard O.W. Mueller** (L.L.M. University of Chicago) was a professor at New York University Law School and director of the Criminal Legal Education and Research Center. Currently on a leave of absence from N.Y.U., he is chief of the United Nations Section on Crime Prevention and Criminal Justice in New York City. Professor Mueller has written extensively in criminology and comparative law including "Crime, Law and the Scholars" (1969) and consulted with numerous government and international organizations.

Paul Nejelski, a graduate of Yale Law School, is currently the Assistant Executive Secretary to the Connecticut Judicial Department and lecturer at the University of Connecticut Law School. At the time of the conference he was director of the Institute of Judicial Administration and an adjunct associate professor at the New York University School of Law. Mr. Nejelski was previously a member of the U.S. Department of Justice for six years, serving as a prosecutor and later as the head of a criminal justice research center. He has coauthored several articles on the need for a scholar's privilege including: "A Researcher-Subject Testimonial Privilege: What to Do

Before the Subpoena Arrives" 1971 *Wisconsin Law Review* 1085 (1971), and "The Prosecutor and the Researcher: Present and Prospective Variations on the Supreme Court's *Branzburg* Decision," 21 *Social Problems* 3 (special issue, 1973).

Howard Peyser, at the time of his co-authorship of the model researchers testimonial privilege statute with Paul Nejelski, was a research associate at the Institute of Judicial Administration and a student at New York University Law School.

Gideon Sjoberg is Professor of Sociology at The University of Texas at Austin. He is author of the *Preindustrial City* (1960) and (co-author with R. Nett) *A Methodology for Social Research* (1968). He is also editor of *Ethics, Politics, and Social Research* (1967) and (co-editor with M.D. Hancock) *Politics in the Post-Welfare States.* He is also editor of a volume in press (with W.B. Littrell) *New Issues in Public Policy* and is in the process of the final editing of a manuscript (co-authored with T.R. Vaughn) on "The Sociology of Ethics."

Marvin E. Wolfgang (Ph.D. University of Pennsylvania) is Professor of Sociology and Law and is director of the Center for Studies in Criminology and Criminal Law at the University of Pennsylvania. Currently president of the American Academy of Political and Social Science, Professor Wolfgang was director of research for the Commission on the Causes and Prevention of Violence. A member of the Panel on Social Indicators for the Department of Health, Education and Welfare, Professor Wolfgang has also been Associate Secretary General and is on the Board of Directors of the International Society of Criminology.